ੴ

FOOTPRINTS IN THE SAND

Gold Coast Sikhs 1980–2020

FOOTPRINTS IN THE SAND

Gold Coast Sikhs 1980–2020

CHAMKAUR SINGH GILL

Australian Scholarly

First published 2020 by
Australian Scholarly Publishing Ltd
7 Lt Lothian St Nth, North Melbourne, Vic 3051
Tel: 03 9329 6963 / Fax: 03 9329 5452
enquiry@scholarly.info / www.scholarly.info

ISBN 978-1-922454-18-8

Cover design: Wayne Saunders

I. Migrant: Footprints

Your footprints fade there,
Even as they deepen here.
Your voice then, a faint echo;
Now heeded, a clarion call.
Your shadow lengthens and grows,
Strengthened by what it used to be.
What you have left behind
Will always cherish you.
What you have embraced
Now nourishes you.

CS Gill

Contents

Preface

The main objective of this book was to document the presence of Sikhs on the Gold Coast dating back to 1980, and, in the process, to examine the role they have played in raising the community's profile through their positive impact on society at large. Contributions were sought from willing participants and then compiled and edited to form a representative cross-section of Sikhs from a variety of walks of life, and from various parts of the world.

The book, which was written over a period of about a year, is mainly based on digital research, one-on-one interviews, individual contributions, anecdotal evidence and the author's personal experiences. An attempt was made to contact as many individuals as possible for Chapter 3; however, due to limited time and resources the result is not a complete representation of the community. Some parties also declined to respond or participate when approached, and others may have been unknown to the author.

Publication was originally scheduled for early 2020, but everything was put on hold because of the global Covid-19 pandemic and the resultant and extended lockdown across the country.

It is hoped that this book succeeds in documenting the history of Gold Coast Sikhs over a stretch of four decades and that it allows future generations to refer to the local Sikh historical narrative in a way the present generation is unable to, given the paucity of information about pre-1980 Sikh residents.

Chamkaur Singh Gill

Gold Coast, Australia

13 July 2020

Acknowledgements

Garland
Behold, a bouquet of such fragrance!
May its fragrance reach far and wide.
Behold, a diamond of reverence!
May its lustre fill us with pride.
Be together, the gentle and the strong.
Adorn with love the land where you belong.

By Mr Joginder Singh Meet.
Translated by his son, Mr Jaswinder Singh.
Edited by Chamkaur Singh Gill.

I would like to express my sincere gratitude to Mr Bhajan Singh Bains for being a sturdy pillar of support, both moral and material, during the creation of this book. His generosity, encouragement and belief in the project served as a major source of inspiration to me, particularly at points when the project was in danger of coming to a standstill.

Special thanks, too, to Mr Maninder (Mannu) Singh Kala for being supportive of this project. His generosity is highly appreciated.

For their generosity, unwavering support and show of faith throughout the process, grateful thanks, too, are due to the following stalwarts who envisioned how meaningful the book would be to the Gold Coast Sikh community, present and future:

Dr Paramjit Singh and family

Mr Ranbir Singh Bhorla and family

Dr Sukhbir Singh Patheja and Mrs Leena Patheja and family

Mr Inder Singh Jaswal and family

Mr Balwinder (Bob) Singh Reehal and family

Mrs Pam Samra and family

Mr Kuldip Singh Kaurah and Mrs Jessy Kaur Kaurah and family

I also wish to record my heartfelt thanks to Mr Benjamin Leadbetter (Illustrator).

In closing, I owe a debt of gratitude to my wife, Bee Chen (Tej Kaur), whose input has been invaluable, and my daughter, Mindy, who has inspired me in this venture. Finally, my thanks to those friends who have supported me with words of encouragement throughout the journey.

1

Sikhs and Sikhism: A Summary

The True One has existed since time immemorial.
He is there today and you will forever find Him there.
He never died nor will He ever die …
Look within, you will see Him there enshrined.

Guru Nanak Dev Ji

The word Sikh means 'disciple' or 'learner' and refers to someone who follows the ethics of Sikhism, a monotheistic religion dating back to the 15th Century CE. Founded in the Punjab, India by Guru Nanak Dev Ji (1439 – 1569), Sikhism now has 30 million adherents globally, making it the ninth-largest religion in the world ('Sikhism', n.d.).

Guru Nanak Dev Ji was succeeded by nine other Gurus. In 1708, Guru Gobind Singh Ji, the tenth Guru, passed on the mantle of Guru to the Sikh Holy Book, the Guru Granth Sahib Ji, which translates to 'The Supreme Enlightener's Revered Scriptures'. In its early form, it was known as the *Adi Granth*, or First Book, and was compiled in 1604 by the fifth Sikh Guru, Guru Arjan Dev Ji. It contained the teachings of the first five Gurus. Guru Gobind Singh Ji added further hymns between 1704 and 1706 and declared that the Guru Granth Sahib Ji would be the final and everlasting living Guru after his death.

The scriptures in the Guru Granth Sahib Ji, which is made up of 1,430 *ang* (pages) and 5,894 *shabad* (poetic compositions), are known as *Gurbani,* meaning 'words of the Guru' or 'words of wisdom'. They appear in the form of devotional poetry and hymns mainly composed by Guru Nanak Ji, Guru Angad Ji, Guru Amar Das Ji, Guru Ram Das Ji, Guru Arjan Ji and Gur Tegh Bahadur Ji, plus devotional poetry by thirteen Hindu saints and two Muslim poets.

A central hymn in the Guru Granth Sahib Ji is the Mool Mantar or Root Chant. It is believed to be the first hymn attributed to Guru Nanak Dev Ji. Effectively, it is '… the entire universally complex theology of the Sikh faith. It has religious, social, political, logical, martial and eternal implications for human existence …' (Sikhiwiki, 2018). These *Gurbani* scriptures form the basis of all Sikh religious ceremonies wherever they are held and represent the *Guru Panth*, or 'path of the Guru', with reference to Sikhs who focus on salvation through devotion to the teachings of the Gurus.

Like all religions, Sikhism is based on consecrated principles to help guide devotees in their daily activities. The three central tenets are devotion to The One God (*Ik Oankaar*) through the recitation of daily prayers, making an honest living, and sharing what one earns. Besides that, Sikhs believe in *seva* (selfless service) for the benefit of others – especially the needy – regardless of faith, ethnicity or position in life, because everyone is equal in the presence of God. It is selfless service in the sense that personal needs and the ego are secondary to applying oneself to the good of others. There is no expectation of reward in the living world. The reward is found when we '… cross over to the other shore' (Guru Nanak Dev Ji). *Seva* is in the form of *mahn,* which means using one's knowledge and mental abilities to assist those in need, *tahn*, which refers to service through physical assistance, and *dhahn*, meaning material help by donating to charitable causes. These philosophies are evident in the following poem by Guru Nanak Dev Ji:

> If people use the wealth bestowed on them by God
> For themselves alone or for treasuring it,

It is like a corpse.
But if they decide to share it with others,
It becomes sacred food.

Sikhs are also expected to live honourable lives and eliminate manifestations of pride, lust, greed, anger and attachment from their lives, which are frowned upon as weaknesses associated with the ego. These five transgressions against spirituality are commonly referred to as *punj chor* or *punj vikar* (five thieves).

The place where Sikhs gather to worship – as a congregation at set assemblies or as individuals at other personal times – is called a Gurdwara, which means 'home of the Guru' or 'door to the Guru'.

A *Nishan Sahib*, or Sikh flag, stands hoisted tall near the entrance of a Gurdwara. It is a saffron-coloured triangular entity with the Sikh symbol *(khanda)* prominently displayed on it. A Gurdwara is configured so that it has four doors (unless it is structurally impossible due to space or design limitations), with one each to represent peace, livelihood, learning and grace and to welcome people from the north, south, east and west. It is open to everyone: Sikh and non-Sikh, poor and rich, and people of all races.

Women or men who step into a Gurdwara are required to cover their head with a turban, handkerchief or shawl, remove footwear and observe proper decorum to demonstrate respect for the religious proceedings and the Guru Granth Sahib Ji. Upon entry, Sikhs are expected to make their way with folded hands to the *takth* (a raised altar for the Holy Book), go down on their knees and touch the floor with their foreheads to depict reverence for the Guru Granth Sahib Ji. Non-Sikhs are welcome to participate in this act of homage if they so choose, although there is no compulsion for them to do so.

The *takth* is generally accompanied by a *palki*, which is a domed structure above the space where the Guru Granth Sahib Ji is placed. After paying obeisance, congregants take their place on the floor with other members of the religious assembly, with no distinction given to social status, race or faith. Those who are unable to sit on the floor because of age or physical disabilities are permitted to sit on chairs at the back or along the sides of the hall. A Gurdwara meditation and prayer ceremony comprises the reading and recitation of Sikh scriptures, *kirtan* (the singing of holy hymns) and sermons by the officiating priest.

Upon conclusion of the spiritual service, all the congregants are invited to the dining section of the Gurdwara for *Guru ka langgar*, which is often shortened to *langgar*. This is a free vegetarian meal during which everyone – male or female, poor or rich – sits side by side on the floor (the physically challenged or elderly can sit at tables) to further strengthen the bonds between Sikh brethren and guests. The concept was introduced by Guru Nanak Dev Ji as a way of promoting equality and creating harmony between people.

The Guru Granth Sahib Ji is treated with great reverence and respect in keeping with its stature as a 'Living Guru'. It should not be placed on the floor or handled with uncleansed hands. Readers should ensure their heads are suitably covered and make sure they do not lick their fingers while turning its pages. It is kept in a special room known as the *Sachkhand*, or 'Domain of Truth', when its scriptures are not being recited, whether at home or in a Gurdwara. While in the *Sachkhand*, it is in *Sukhaasan,* meaning 'Peaceful Repose'. In the morning, it goes through the *Prakaash,* or 'Awakening Ceremony', when the Guru Granth Sahib Ji's *Saroop*, or 'Being', is moved from the *Sachkhand* to the place of prayer. At night, it is respectfully returned to the *Sachkhand* for *Sukhaasan*. Both the morning and night ceremonies are accompanied by the *Ardaas*, meaning 'Prayer', to show devotion to God. The *Ardaas* for the *Prakaash* is recited after 5 *Banis*, or scriptures, have been rendered. These five *Banis* are *Japji Sahib, Jaap Sahib, Amrit Savaiye, Benti Chaupai* and *Anand Sahib*. In the case of *Sukhaasan*, the *Ardaas* comes after *Rehraas Sahib* and *Kirtan Sohila*.

Sikh names are based on Gurmukhi, an early language that originated in the Punjab. The literal meaning of Gurmukhi is 'from the mouth of the Guru'. Punjabi, the language used in the Punjab, is a variation of Gurmukhi in its original form. Gurmukhi was formalised by the second Sikh Guru, Guru Angad Dev Ji, and used by him in the 16th Century to document his hymns and those of Guru Nanak Dev Ji. All the Sikh scriptures in the Guru Granth Sahib Ji are written in Gurmukhi and names for newborn Sikh babies and Sikh converts are selected from this Holy Book. A male Sikh has Singh, meaning 'lion', as his second name while a female Sikh's second name is Kaur, which translates to 'princess'. In the case of the latter, though, it is common to find women who have their fathers' surname, Singh, as their own surname. Some examples are mentioned in this book. This can be attributed to the Western convention whereby daughters and sons take on paternal surnames.

In the Sikh faith, males and females, regardless of their status, ethnic backgrounds and faith, are considered to have equal rights at home and in society. As such, it is not uncommon to find female priests conducting prayer ceremonies side by side with male priests.

Sikhism is not a religion that overtly seeks to convert non-Sikhs, preferring instead to let its all-encompassing philosophies and practices associated with life and spirituality speak for themselves. It respects every religion that praises God as the One Almighty Being and encourages adherents of each faith to observe the teachings of their own denomination diligently. Having stated that, if there are interested parties who wish to embrace the Sikh religion, they are initiated into the faith through a holy *Amrit Sanchar* (also referred to as *Amrit Shakan* and *Amrit Sanskar*) ceremony. This ceremony is attributed to Guru Gobind Singh Ji, who introduced it in 1699 in the process of establishing the *Khalsa*. The *Khalsa* refers mainly to Sikhs who completely immerse themselves in Sikhism.

Practising Sikhs who have been baptised possess five specific identifications that start with the Punjabi equivalent of the 'K' sound, namely *kesh* (unshorn head, facial and body hair), *karra* (steel bangle), *kashera* (under-shorts), *kirpan* (a symbolic sheathed dagger), and *kangga* (a comb to keep their hair tidy). Together, they are known as the *panj kakkar* and serve as a daily reminder of what the *Khalsa* stands for. To keep the hair on the head tidy, Sikh men wear a *dastaar*, or turban. Sikhism is the only religion in the world that requires its practising male followers to wear a turban as an article of faith. In the case of female Sikhs, wearing a turban is optional.

When Sikhs greet each other, they normally fold their hands, palms together, and say *'Sat Sri Akaal'*, meaning 'God is the Great Truth'. This greeting is used both formally, for example, when meeting another Sikh for the first time, and informally with family and Sikh friends. Another widely used greeting, palms together, is *'Vaheguru Ji Ka Khalsa, Vaheguru Ji Ki Fateh'*, which means 'The Khalsa belongs to God, God rewards with victory' and is commonly used when addressing a gathering. Congregants also fold their hands in Gurdwaras at the end of a prayer session, after the priest has recited the *Ardaas*. Everyone who is physically able stands up during this prayer. The priest then closes the prayer ceremony with the declaration, *'Jo Bolay So Nihaal . . .'*, which means, 'Blessed are they who say . . .', followed by *'Sat Sri Akaal'* from the entire congregation.

Like all religions that place a significant value on morals, conventional Sikhism teaches Sikhs of the *Khalsa* to avoid the moral degeneration that can arise from unwanted or taboo beliefs and practices. Cutting, trimming or shaving hair from the head, face or body, pre-marital sex, adultery, and intoxicants like alcohol and drugs fall into this category. Tobacco is also strictly forbidden, as is the consumption of meat from animals killed through sacrificial rituals, because of the suffering experienced by the animals.

In addition, the worship of idols, deities and humans is frowned upon, as it clashes with the concept of *Ik Oankaar* (one God). Sikhs are also advised to reject the notion of the superiority of one group over another, whether according to race, status, caste or gender, and to respect everyone equally. Superstitions are also anathema to followers of Sikhism; Sikhs should not subscribe to superstitions associated with numerology, astrology or meaningless rituals. The underlying philosophy is that the One God is all, and superstitions have the effect of detracting followers from the spirituality of *Ik Oankaar*

Sikhism is the world's youngest organised religion, with philosophies that are highly relevant to modern times, including ideas around gender equality. Women are no less integral to society than men because, in the words of Guru Nanak Dev Ji, '... we are bound with the world through women. Why should we talk ill of her, who gives birth to kings? The woman is born from woman; there is none without her ...' In fact, Sikhism's principle of inclusiveness encompasses all the people of the world. This inclusiveness manifests itself in diverse ways, including welcoming all of humanity and providing selfless service where it is needed, regardless of whom the recipients are.

II. Migrant: The Will in You

From your land of five rivers,
You crossed the seven seas.
Taking what life delivers,
Never brought to your knees.

Your strong calloused hand
Harvests earth's sweetness.
You travel the gritty land,
Bringing far-flung souls gladness.

No companion but your horse.
No wayside home but your cart.
Misty eyes flicker over the source
Still evoking the beat of your heart.

Plunderers ignore your worth.
Inconsequential subordinate.
Vetoed brotherhood at birth.
High colour, pigmentation and hate.

How the will in you prevails!
One Truth in the face of abhorrence.
Your steel is described in tales
Of valour, bloodshed and sufferance.

And when they see your courage,
Their loathing turns into acclaim.
Your dignity, your carriage,
Your mettle – they honour your name.

CS Gill

2

A Brief History of Sikhs in Australia

With your own hands carve out your destiny.

Guru Nanak Dev Ji

Sikhs can be found all over the world today, in countries as diverse as China, Iceland or Botswana, with the largest numbers outside India residing in North America and the United Kingdom. Many are recent migrants but the residents in these countries also include descendants of Sikh migrants who left their homeland, the Punjab in India, generations ago.

In Australia, the Sikh history can be traced back to the 1830s and 1840s, when Sikhs first arrived to work as farmhands, hawkers (Tewari, 2014), cameleers and gold miners (Copp and Booth, 2017). The Sikh immigration was linked to the colonial presence of the British in India and Australia; British penal colonies were being abolished and labour vacancies were created when convicts were no longer forced to do manual labour (All About Sikhs, n.d.).

Today, Sikhs are an integral part of Australian society, firmly ensconced in professional careers far removed from their early days of struggle, which allows them to give back to the nation that adopted them almost 200 years ago.

2.1 Early Sikh Arrivals

According to Kenna and Jordan (2015c), Dabee Singh and his wife, Nunkey Kaur, arrived in Australia in 1844 (see *2.4 Australian roots: Pooran Dabee-Singh*), and were among the first recorded Sikhs to make the migration. However, other sources indicate that Sikhs looking for jobs first arrived in the 1830s to satisfy the demand for agrarian labour ('Sikhism in Australia', n.d.). Their numbers increased from around 1860 when many young Sikhs from the farms of Punjab came to Australia to work as agricultural labourers and hawkers (McCarthy, 2013) in New South Wales, Queensland, Victoria, South Australia and Western Australia. A few also joined the gold rush in Victoria.

The early Sikhs of Australia have been given limited prominence in recorded history. This is the case despite the contribution Sikhs made to Australia's development, particularly in agriculture, labour, and the hawker trade, which helped supply remote areas with much-needed food and household supplies.

Aside from limited personal accounts of individual Sikh migrants, there is inadequate documentary evidence of early Australian Sikh lifestyles and communities, making it difficult to build a composite or substantial picture of those early years. Written records tended to focus on individuals and matters pertaining to white society, with brief, insignificant or unflattering mentions of non-white residents. Existing perfunctory narratives about Sikh exploits as farmhands, hawkers, pedlars or wrestlers do little to identify them as relevant players in Australia's early history.

This lack of information could be attributed to two probable reasons. Firstly, they could have been classified as foreign sojourners who came to Australia looking for employment but who were only fit for manual labour – it was assumed that they would return to India once they had made enough money to support their families back home. The other, more likely reason was that the British colonialists viewed non-white groups of people as being of a lower calibre than white people. Indeed, the Adelaide *Register* in 1893 described them as '... the scum and offscouring of the earth', while

L. F. Benaud, the editor of New South Wales *Richmond River Times* '... harshly declared in 1896 that "no greater pest is to be met in the country than the objectionable dirty Hindoo hawkers who infest many districts"' (Allen, 2008). The term 'Hindoo' was a generic term often used erroneously by the British at the time to identify all Indians. Seen in this light, the Sikh hawkers would have been considered largely unimportant from a social perspective and, therefore, not worth writing about expansively.

This attitude was probably exacerbated by the history of the all-powerful British East India Company in India, which dated back to the 18th Century. The company perpetuated an uncharitable view of Indians, particularly unskilled manual workers or farmhands who were relegated to menial or unappealing work and thought of as fit only to fill gaps left by white workers who might have moved on to other, more salubrious vocations.

Sikh migrants who believed firmly in the Guru Granth Sahib Ji message that all humans are equal in the eyes of God most likely viewed the colonial assumption of white superiority with a deep sense of discomfort. This fundamental cultural difference would have been particularly apparent when the first Prime Minister of Australia, Edmund Barton, signalled the early aspirations of monoculturalism and the White Australia Policy by stating in 1901 that non-whites were '... in comparison with white races ... unequal and inferior' (Jones, 2017).

Where written records did exist, Sikhs were often identified as Afghan Muslims and their names were altered randomly (for example, Otim instead of Utam, Siva instead of Sewa, Croppo instead of Karpal, Sing instead of Singh), or they were given 'pet' names like Jackie or Johnny (Staley, 2015). This was further evidence of the lack of inclusiveness the ruling authorities and white settlers had for non-white migrant communities; a sense of 'us and them' prevailed.

The case of Croppo Sing, whose actual name may have been Karpal Singh, is an example of this prevalent cultural indifference. Although he made history on 11 March 1848 by becoming the first customer of The Savings Bank of South Australia (now known as BankSA), when he deposited his savings of £29, his name was recorded as Croppo Sing, with his ethnicity listed as Afghan ('Our Story', n.d.).

Of course, it is possible that the names of these arrivals, who spoke and wrote little or no English, were written down on a phonetic basis, or that it was relatively easy to mistake them for Afghans. However, these discrepancies could have been avoided if the British registering officials had been more diligent and less dismissive of cultures other than their own.

Going on these assumptions, it is highly likely that the involvement of non-white migrants like the Sikhs and other Indians in decision-making processes was incidental or severely limited. A few exceptions, as mentioned in the coming pages, were the experiences of Putarb Singh, Siva Singh, Bud Singh, Massa Singh and Pooran Dabee-Singh.

2.2 Sikh Cameleers, Pedlars and Hawkers

Before the era of modern roads and railway tracks, transporting food and materials to the interior of Australia was dependent on camels to a significant extent. Cameleers played an essential role in distributing supplies to remote farms and mines, which in turn set the stage for the future development of isolated parts of Australia and the advancement of an emerging nation.

Most of the cameleers, as they were known, were Afghans, but a number of Sikhs were also recruited to handle the camels. These Sikh cameleers were often referred to as Afghans or Ghans, most likely because of their similarity in appearance (they both wore turbans and beards), and the lack of knowledge on the part of the Australian authorities about the difference between the two ethnic groups.

The Burke and Wills Expedition (1860–61) from Melbourne to the Gulf of Carpentaria may also point to the presence of Sikh cameleers in Australia at that time, given that there were camels named Golah Sing and Bell Sing in the expedition (Burke and Wills Web Digital Research Archive, n.d.). As mentioned, the name Sing was often used as a misnomer in place of Singh, and while it is important to note that the surname (or middle name) Singh is not restricted to Sikhs alone – it is also found in non-Sikh communities, such as Rajput Hindus and other North-Indian Hindus – Sikhs formed a large proportion of mid- to late-nineteenth-century Indian migrants ('Indian Australians', n.d.). Therefore, it is fair to assume that the names Singh and Sing belonged to Sikhs (Sikh Interfaith Council of Australia, n.d.).

A few Sikh cameleers eventually became camel owners, such as Pal Singh (Sikh Interfaith Council of Victoria [APA], n.d.). Pal Singh was recorded in the 1880s as one of the earliest cameleers in Wyndham (History Teachers' Association of WA [APA], n.d.).

In addition to being camel handlers, some Sikhs also became hawkers and pedlars. They started monopolising the hawking trade from the 1890s when they were given licences that were reserved for British subjects, thereby denying Afghan, Chinese and other non-British migrant traders similar opportunities (All About Sikhs, n.d.).

The hawkers travelled from place to place on foot or in their horse-drawn carts to sell supplies to remote farms, households and workplaces. As with the cameleers, the part they played in the early development of modern Australia was significant. These mobile Sikh traders '... were often represented as being of great assistance to outlying settlements and welcome friends at scattered farms' (Allen, 2008).

An extract from a book written by Alison Muir (Settler Footprints from Star: Muir Family – Pioneers of the South West and Eucla, Western Australia, 1844–2005) in an online article by the Australian Sikh Heritage describes how two Sikh hawker brothers, Herman (probably Harman) Singh and Nehal Singh, would delight adults and children alike every time they visited. The extract refers to the hawkers' 'kindly nature' and the 'treasures' they brought with them, including '... blankets, dress lengths, cottons, ribbons, shoelaces, wool, needles, socks, trousers, tea, matches, soaps, pocket knives, working boots, slippers ...'. It also describes how they shared their bannocks and johnny cakes (most likely Punjabi chappatis) and lentil curry with the children ('Nehal Singh, Herman Singh and Sundah Singh', 2014).

Some of these travelling hawkers turned out to be quite successful in their trade. For example, a hawker named Otim (probably Uttam) Singh became the owner of a store called People's Store on Kangaroo Island, South Australia, in the early 1900s (Sikh Interfaith Council of Victoria). He married a white woman named Susannah Buick and they both settled in Kingscote, where Otim eventually earned a measure of respect despite the prevailing racism (Aly, 2013). His customers included the people of Kingscote and local farmers. Business was especially good during the summer holidays and he was able to expand his store over time. He was so successful that he was mentioned in the *Cyclopedia of South Australia* in 1909 (Allen, 2008).

Putarb (probably Purtarb or Partaap) Singh was another early migrant Sikh who made a name for himself in New South Wales. He arrived in Australia in 1884 at the age of 19 and became a travelling hawker and horse dealer. He also ventured successfully into selling used goods, earning the nickname Cheap Jack Charley for his ability to '… resell anything that stood, or even leaned, on four legs'. (Kenna & Jordan, 2015a). Through hard work, Putarb became quite wealthy and, in addition to having almost £1000 in the local bank, he was the owner of two houses in Henty, where he lived for about fifty years. He was something of a colourful person, with whiskers long enough to be stretched and tied at the back of his head. It is believed that he signed a petition in May 1902 requesting the Australian Government allow a member to be elected to represent Indian interests in relation to the White Australia Policy (officially known as the Immigration Restrictive Act 1901).

Putarb Singh died in 1951 and came to be known as the last Sikh in Henty that year. It has been suggested that he committed suicide because of mental health issues (Kenna & Jordan, 2015a). The police believed that he had set his home on fire and cut his own throat, although there is no clear evidence to support this. It is worth noting that, although in life he had seen to it that Sikhs who had passed away were given proper funeral rites involving cremations, he himself was buried in an unmarked grave in the Henty Cemetery. Fortunately, the authorities later managed to identify his grave and place a marker on it.

Siva (probably Sewa) Singh was another Sikh migrant who started as a hawker and became a wealthy person. He arrived in Australia in 1886 or 1887 and worked as a hawker in the Benalla District, Victoria. He soon purchased a horse-drawn wagon to extend his trade. Among the everyday items he sold were shoes he had acquired from Australian shoemakers like Whybrow & Co Pty Ltd (Kenna and Jordan, 2020). His abandoned wagon, with '... secret compartments containing snippets of Mr Singh's life: empty cans of curry, children's shoes and rates notices' (Lee, 2020), was discovered in a shed by researchers Crystal Jordan and Len Kenna. The wagon is expected to be put on permanent display as an indicator of the role played by him and other Sikh hawkers who helped supply remote areas with much-needed goods.

By 1915, after years of hard work and frugal living, Siva Singh was the owner of an acreage grazing property and farm in Benalla. His legacy lies in two major events. One was an *Akhand Paatth* (an extended prayer ceremony that involves the reading of the Guru Granth Sahib in its entirety) that was held on the grounds of his property on 16 December 1920, with the Australian flag and Union Jack flanking the Guru Granth Sahib. The flags denoted Siva's respect for the new land he lived in. He presided over the ceremony, which was considered to have been the first *Akhand Paatth* held in Australia, as the *Granthi* (Sikh priest). The second event that gave him a place in Australian history was regaining the right to vote in 1925 (having lost it in 1915 because of the White Australia Policy) after a ten-year legal battle (Lee, 2020). Such an achievement classifies him as an early Sikh equal-rights fighter in Australia.

A monument erected by Benalla Council to Siva Singh's legacy was unveiled in November 2019. Crystal Jordan and Ken Lee, together with the Australian-Indian Historical Society (Lee, 2020), played an important role in this recognition of a Sikh Australian pioneer.

Another early Sikh migrant worth noting was Bud (or Budh) Singh who came to Australia in 1899. He started out as a hawker who travelled to his customers carrying his wares in a basket perched on his head. He soon made enough money to purchase a horse-drawn cart. Bud was very diligent, hard-working and thrifty and eventually went from being a struggling foot-hawker to achieving financial security through investment in the silver-mining industry and as a successful store owner in Yerranderie (Ahmad, 2014).

Bud was, apparently, quite vigorous in putting forward his views, being a person of great self-belief. Despite his demanding personality, he donated generously to the Red Cross Society and the local hospital, in keeping with his Sikh beliefs of service and sharing. Consequently, the Board of the Camden Hospital in New South Wales honoured him with life membership (Singh, 2014b). He received this honour in 1919, followed soon after with a plaque. For some reason best known to the Camden hospital authorities, the plaque disappeared during renovations. It was largely due to the persistence of Sydney resident Mr Baljinder Singh, with the assistance of Len Kenna and Crystal Jordan of the Australian-Indian Historical Society and other prominent members of the community, that the Camden Hospital agreed to have a new plaque made to commemorate Bud Singh (Ahmad, 2014). Bud's high profile also led to his being invited to present cycling, athletics and rifle club medals and awards. He was quite prosperous by the time he returned to India in 1926 (Ahmad, 2014), leaving behind freehold land in Yerranderie, which was sold at an official auction in 1952 (Singh, 2014a).

Another prominent Sikh was Baba Ram Singh, who arrived in Australia in 1898. He is believed to have brought the first Guru Granth Sahib Ji to Australia in the 1920s ('Sikhism in Australia', n.d.). Baba Ram Singh was a Bangalow resident and travelled in a horse-drawn cart to surrounding areas, selling fruit and vegetables. He laid the foundation stone for Australia's first Sikh Gurdwara in Woolgoolga, (History Teachers' Association of WA [APA], n.d.) at the age of around 92. Baba Ram Singh passed away in 1983 at the age of 106.

Massa Singh, who arrived in Fremantle, West Australia, in 1896, was a celebrated West Australian Sikh in the early 1900s, especially in the field of wrestling. At least two of his fights, which he won against wrestlers named Pearce and Watson, were reported in the local press (Grewal, 2016). His victory against Pearce earned him £100, while his victory against Watson gave him the title of Australian Champion – a title that he held for 161 days (Kenna and Jordan, 2014a).

Massa Singh was also a cameleer but, unlike Afghan cameleers who came as low-paid indentured workers struggling to make a living in poor working conditions, Massa worked independently and leased out his services as a Private Cartage Contractor (Kenna and Jordan, 2014c). As a cameleer, he is noted for having taken his contractors, H Francisco and Peter Epis, to court in May 1922 for unpaid wages amounting to £122.12, which he was owed for the transportation of copper and other goods between March and August 1920. He won the case with costs in June 1922 (Kenna and Jordan, 2014c). He was also known for having been appointed a trustee, together with Bulla (probably Bhola) Singh, of West Australia's first officially recognised Sikh crematorium at Canning River Flat in 1932 (Kenna & Jordan, 2015a).

Buttan Singh, who arrived in Western Australia in 1900, was another Sikh wrestler to gain fame. He became the first winner of the Australian Wrestling Champion title by defeating Gunga Brahm on May 2, 1903, and later won titles in The United States of America and Great Britain. In addition, he was among the world's best at swinging 6.3-kilogram clubs (History Teachers' Association of WA [APA], n.d.). His physical prowess and grip were so powerful that it is believed he was able to swing a pair of nail-studded clubs weighing about 20 kilograms for an hour, 36-kilogram clubs 50 times continuously, and 45-kilogram clubs 20 times (Wood, 2018).

2.3 A New Home

Among the white settler population, there was widespread discrimination against new migrants, particularly those who were non-Caucasian. For example, Sikhs were referred to as 'Black and turbaned heathens' by the editor of the Richmond River Times in 1895 (McCarthy, 2013, p. 76). In the case of Siva Singh, who was mentioned previously, a local newspaper in Benalla referred to him as an 'aboriginal native of Asia' during the court case to have his voting rights reinstated (Lee, 2020). The words implied that Siva Singh (and, by implication, other Indians) was equivalent to the poorly treated Indigenous Australians and, therefore, inferior to whites. This open racism, combined with the generally solitary nature of their work resulted in '... prolonged social isolation and psychological trauma', which, in turn, led to suicides and suicide attempts (Spennemann, 2019).

However, after World War I, Sikhs were looked upon a bit more generously. This was mainly because a few Sikh soldiers had fought alongside British and ANZAC (Australian and New Zealand Army Corps) troops during the war ('Sikhism in Australia', n.d.). There were at least 21 Sikhs in the Australian Imperial Force, two of whom were killed in action in Belgium: Private Nain Singh Sailani and Private Sarn (probably Saran) Singh (Adams, n.d.).

Some of the Sikh soldiers served as gunners and mule drivers and performed heroically. According to a Lance-Corporal Neeld, every single one of them deserved a Victoria Cross (Bedi and Bedi, 2017). There is also mention of a soldier named Narain Singh who repaired phone lines. He was the only lineman available and, despite heavy fire, repaired lines to ensure that essential communication channels were kept open (Bedi and Bedi, 2017).

A little-known fact is that Sikhs also served as medical personnel during World War I. Dr Waryam Singh, the grandfather of Gold Coast resident Dr Avtar Singh Gill, was a medical officer who '...served in the Sikh Regiment with British and ANZAC officers in Egypt, Palestine and Turkey in 1915 and tended to the injured soldiers including ANZACs, Sikhs and others' (Gill, 2013). After the war, the Australian government had a soft spot for Sikhs because of heroic episodes like these, which put them in a preferred position above other non-whites when it came to awarding special privileges (All About Sikhs, n.d.). They could own land, had the right to vote, could secure hawking licences, and were given pensions. These privileges, however, did not mean they were treated as equals by white Australians. The '… vilification and marginalisation by the Australian community, which was jealous of their hard-working attitudes …' remained an ongoing problem (Spennemann, 2019).

Although Sikhs faced fewer hurdles than other non-white migrants in moving their sons from India to Australia, by and large, the Australian authorities were not keen for their families to join them ('Sikhism in Australia', n.d.). With the commencement of the White Australia Policy in 1901, migration of non-whites came to a virtual standstill. Would-be migrants, the vast majority of whom probably knew no language other than their own, were required to take an absurd dictation test in which they had to write 50 words based on a random European language. Officers administering it '… could manipulate the test to exclude any undesired person' (Jones, 2017). In this case, 'undesired person' referred to a non-European and failure meant deportation (National Archives of Australia, n.d.).

Some eventually returned to the Punjab permanently (Sikh Interfaith Council of Victoria [APA], n.d.), possibly the victims of this obstacle. Others managed to secure the Certificate of Exemption to the Dictation Test (CEDT) that excused them from having to take it but they had to have been in Australia before 1900. An additional obstacle was that they had to return to their homeland after procuring the CEDT but could come back to Australia later and live here without having to take the test (Kenna and Jordan, 2016).

2.4 Australian Roots: Pooran Dabee-Singh

Pooran Dabee-Singh was born in 1849 in the Burnett District in Queensland and may have been one of the first Australian-born Sikhs, if not the first, whose parents were both migrants from the Punjab. His father, Dabee (possibly Dalbir) Singh, and mother, Nunkey (probably Naanki) Kaur, are thought to have been among the earliest recorded Sikh migrants to Australia, having arrived by sea on 28 October 1844 together with 23 other indentured workers from India. They were hired to work as domestic help in Brisbane at a monthly rate of 50 cents but ended up as shepherds and hut keepers in Ipswich. Their misfortune did not end there – they suffered the humiliation of '… being whipped and being supplied with insufficient rations' (Kenna and Jordan, 2014b) while in Ipswich.

Kenna and Jordan (2015c) note that Pooran received his education at the Normal School and St. John's School in Brisbane. He had an interest in horses and, like his father, became a keen horse-businessman. He used his know-how to start a Royal Mail and Passenger Service to Cleveland. He also transported boat skippers from Pinkenba to Brisbane and back.

Pooran's good nature was in evidence when he helped a competitor, whom he had previously put out of business, start a new venture. He had a knack for curing sick or injured animals and created a treatment that he called *Marchee Tael*, a Punjabi term that means 'chilli oil', though there is no record of whether it worked or not. Pooran's reputation with horses led to his being invited to be a judge at horse shows. In addition, he introduced horse-trotting races to Brisbane and turned out to be quite a good horse-trotter himself. In his final race in the 1880s, he beat the required completion time by nine seconds and won one thousand pounds (Kenna and Jordan, 2015c).

Pooran married Elizabeth Goodall, the daughter of the owner of the Brighton Hotel, and later purchased it from his father-in-law, a sign of his business acuity. He also owned a variety of other properties, including quite a few farms (Kenna and Jordan, 2015c).

During World War I, Pooran donated generously to different causes and contributed to the coordination of efforts between the Australian and Indian governments. His suggestions were valid enough for them to be adopted by India and for him to get a letter of thanks from King George V (Kenna and Jordan, 2015c). He also leased Grange Hill, a property he owned, to the Red Cross during the war. Ever ready to speak his mind, he complained to the Premier of Queensland, Thomas Ryan, in 1919 about the lack of job opportunities in the sugar-cane industry for Indian workers as compared to similar opportunities for German workers (Kenna and Jordan 2015c).

Pooran Dabee-Singh died in Brisbane in 1927. As there was no existing crematorium in Brisbane (it was not until 1934 that Queensland's first crematorium was opened), he was buried in the Toowong Cemetery, leaving behind his widow, three children and three grandchildren. Two of his descendants – his great-grandson Frederic Robert Hamilton Singh and his great-grand-daughter Margaret Helen Hamilton Singh – served in the Royal Australian Airforce during World War II (Kenna and Jordan, 2015c).

2.5 Australian Roots: Bung Singh

Some early Sikh migrants put down roots in Australia and married local Indigenous women. One such person was Bung (possibly Bhag) Singh, a hawker who traded around the Tammin and Yorkrakine Rock areas of Western Australia (Singh, 2018c). He married an Indigenous woman sometime in the 1870s and, as it turned out, was the grandfather of the late Jack Davis MBE AM, a renowned poet, playwright and activist. Jack Davis identified himself as a Sikh on at least one occasion – in 1977 or 1978 he greeted the late Dr Amarjeet Singh, a founding member of the Australian Sikh Heritage Association (ASHA), with *Sat Sri Akal* and went on to mention his religious background (Grewal, 2017). There are probably numerous similar cases of Sikh men marrying both Indigenous and non-Indigenous women in the early years of Sikh migration. Research on the links between Sikhs and Indigenous Australians conducted by Dya Singh, a famed *Gurbani* singer, refers to his discoveries in little townships where some locals had 'Singh' as their surnames and showed him photographs of early Sikh migrants (Singh, 2020).

2.6 Australian Roots: Mahan Singh, Bhagwan Singh and Tara Singh

Australian-born Gold Coast resident Janette Singh can also trace her roots back to the early days of Sikh migration to Australia in the 1800s. According to Janette's daughter, Priya Singh, Janette's great-grandfather, Sardar Mahan Singh, stepped foot on Australian soil in 1885 and made the Atherton Tablelands, Queensland, his place of residence. As was the case with most migrants, he came alone, while his wife, Radha Kaur, remained in India.

Mahan worked in Teven, New South Wales, as a corn-picker and in Mclean as a sugar-cane harvester for five- to six-month stretches. He was more educated than many other Indian labourers and, as a result, they would turn to him to help them write letters home.

Most migrant labourers returned to India after earning enough money to provide for their families, though some did come back to Australia for further employment. Mahan Singh was no different; he went home after working for about three years in Australia on his first visit.

Mahan Singh's son, Bhagwan Singh (who was married to Eshar Kaur) arrived in Australia in 1901 by ship. It did not take him long to realise that he was risking arrest and deportation due to the White Australia Policy, so to avoid detection and arrest he travelled to his destination during the night. On arrival, Bhagwan Singh discovered that there were few opportunities available for employment. Undeterred, he accepted any employment opportunity that came his way, including corn-picking.

Bhagwan Singh had three sons, Nasib Singh, Teja Singh and Tara Singh Grewal (Janette Singh's father). Tara was born in 1926 in India and married Gian Kaur (a woman he had been promised to at a young age, in keeping with Indian marriage customs of the time) in 1944. Gian was born in 1927 and in her teenage years she often spent time learning to cook in preparation for her marriage to Tara.

Tara came to Australia in 1947 to undertake work in the Atherton Tablelands on a peanut farm. At the time, the going wage was approximately £2 per day. Following this, Tara cut sugarcane for two years at Red Lynch with his brother Nasib Singh. The brothers lived in simple barracks that were constructed for farmers to live in. With his earnings, Tara travelled to India to build a house for his family before returning to Australia.

On his second trip to Australia, Tara resumed his work as a sugarcane labourer. When the seasonal sugar-cane work ended, he travelled to Murwillumbah to work on a banana farm for a period of two years. However, the wage of approximately three shillings per hour was insufficient for his needs and this led Tara to return to cane-cutting work when it became available.

In 1949, Tara ventured away from his brothers to move to Gordonvale in Cairns, Far North Queensland. He was accompanied by two of his Muslim friends, Galama and Bishna. In 1954, Tara's wife joined him from India and they lived in Little Mulgrave. At that time, the White Australia Policy was still in force and non-Europeans were not allowed privileges that whites enjoyed. For example, unlike in Murwillumbah, there were occasions when non-whites in Cairns received limited or no service at outlets that sold alcohol. Tara began work as a tobacco-picker during the 1960s in Mareeba and Dimboola, and when employment was scarce he worked for the council and on the railways.

Tara and Gian had their eldest child Robyn in 1956. The couple went on to have five other children: Janette (born in 1958), Robert (1960), John (1961), Raymond (1965) and Sharon (1967). John Singh Grewal was born in India while the other siblings were born in Australia.

It is interesting to note that the siblings were given their first names by their mother with the aid of a white nurse. The names were western-oriented and showed a desire on the part of their mother to help her children assimilate more easily into western society. Indeed, there are numerous cases of Sikhs today who adopt western-sounding nicknames like Jack, Sam and Bill because their names are tongue-twisters to non-Punjabi ears. Perhaps the experiences of their forefathers, as explained in Chapter 2.1, convinced them of the need to go to these lengths. (A few examples are mentioned in Chapter 3.) A no-fuss transition like this is indicative of a group of people who are happy to be part of an ongoing process of integration.

Janette Singh grew up in Gordonvale, North Queensland, before arriving in Woolgoolga, New South Wales, in 1971 and commencing high school with her siblings. She noticed that she and her family faced less discrimination there than in their previous town of residence, probably due to the larger Indian population. This was the case both within the community and, specifically, in the local school.

After they relocated, Janette's parents bought a 27-acre banana plantation on which the elder siblings would work every weekend and some mornings before school to make ends meet. She packed the bananas and, after her sister married and moved away, took on the additional task of harvesting.

In 1976, she began her employment in Pacific Film Laboratories working for Jim Reid and Irwin Ellem. Janette worked there for approximately six years until the company closed and then found work under Gary Leech at the Camera House store in Park Beach Plaza, Coffs Harbour, until 1989.

In April 1988, Janette sponsored and married her fiancé, Dr Hargurdip Singh. He arrived in Australia from India two weeks before they were to be married. In October 1989, they moved to Melbourne where he commenced training to get his Indian medical degree recognised in Australia, with his wife's continued support.

In December 1993, they moved to Mildura, Victoria where their first daughter, Pavanjit Singh, was born in May that year. Dr Hargurdip Singh worked for a year in Mildura Base Hospital in Obstetrics and Gynaecology. Janette and Hargurdip found Mildura to be quite different from Melbourne, being a regional town. The end of 1995 saw the couple return to Melbourne. They then decided to relocate to Newcastle, New South Wales, in the hope of finding a place to live that was farther up the coast to be closer to their extended family. A year later in 1997, they made the move to the Gold Coast where they reside today and where their second daughter, Priya, was born in 1999.

2.7 Australian Roots: Gurdit Singh

Gurdit Singh was the father of Rajwans Kaur Samra, a Gold Coast resident of many years. He came to Australia in 1920 and worked in Bendigo, Victoria, for four years before entering the hawking trade with a horse-drawn cart. He was a hawker from 1924 to 1963. His wife, Surjit Kaur, joined him in Australia in 1930.

Gurdit was one of a dwindling number of mobile traders who travelled to remote areas around Bendigo, supplying everyday necessities like food, water, clothing, homewares and equipment to families of farmers and villagers. Eventually, with the advent of modern roads and railways, horse-drawn-cart peddling ceased to exist.

Gurdit Singh's role in the history of Bendigo was significant enough for him to be mentioned in the Bendigo library records.

2.8 Punjaub and Malwa

There is ample and compelling evidence that Sikhs have left a significant mark on the Queensland landscape. For example, in Northern Queensland there is an area of 715 square kilometres called Punjaub, an obvious variation of Punjab. Punjaub was given its name in 1877 by an Indian-born Englishman, Sydney Watson (Singh, 2018b), possibly due to the presence of Sikh migrant farmhands in the area or due to the five rivers flowing through it –the Punjab also has five rivers flowing through it and is often called 'land of five rivers'. Punjaub has cattle stations and parishes with names like Ravi and Chenab, which are likewise names of rivers that flow through the Punjab. Further local places like Doab, Little Doab, Almora and Indus also have names that reference India (Singh, 2018b).

In the 1880s, Punjaub was renowned for its important cattle station and its production of fruit of various kinds, including citrus, mangoes and bananas. The area is also significant to Indigenous people, as evidenced by the fact that some of them carry the surname Punjaub (Singh, 2018a).

Farther south in the North Gregory district of Queensland, there is a county named Malwa, which seems to be a direct reference to the Malwa region in the Punjab (Singh, 2018b), and further reinforces the impact of the Sikh presence in this part of Queensland.

2.9 Latter-Day Sikh Australians

The 2016 Census of Population and Housing conducted by the Australian Bureau of Statistics lists Sikhism as the fifth largest religion in Australia, with almost 125,909 adherents (Singh, 2017). This figure, compared to that of 1996, when there were only 12,000 Sikhs ('Sikhism in Australia', n.d.), is a clear indicator of the interest Sikhs have in living in Australia. Other figures provided by the Bureau indicate that, between 2011 and 2016, the Sikh population grew by 74%, making it the fastest growing religion in Australia ('Census reveals Australia's religious diversity on World Religion Day', 2018).

Sikhs have migrated to Australia not just to build comfortable lifestyles for themselves and their families but also to contribute to the economic wellbeing of the country. A 2016 report revealed that Sikh migrants contributed significantly to the wealth of Australia, adding $8.1 billion to the country's coffers annually (Arora and Singh, 2019). This achievement is evidence of their commitment to hard work and productivity. Matt Kean, New South Wales Minister for Innovation and Better Regulation, put it succinctly in 2017 when he praised the contributions of Sikh Australians by saying, 'I do not think you will find a better, more decent, more hardworking group of migrants ... They have made Australia the great country which it is' (Merani, 2017).

Today, Sikhs can be found all over Australia, with Woolgoolga (in New South Wales) an important focal point for them. Although there are more Sikhs in cities like Melbourne, Sydney and Brisbane, Woolgoolga is historically noteworthy to Sikh Australians because it was where they first started settling down in increasing numbers, especially from the 1940s onwards. According to a 2016 report by the Australian Bureau of Statistics, there were 840 Sikhs in Woolgoolga that year, out of a total population of 5,290 people ('2016 Census QuickStats' 2016). It is also the place where the first Australian Gurdwara was built.

The history of Woolgoolga Sikhs is on display at the Sikh Heritage Museum of Australia located on River Street. This museum also depicts the wider Australian and international history of Sikhs and showcases wide-ranging aspects of religion and culture associated with Sikhism.

On the Gold Coast, a 2016 census lists Surfers Paradise as home to 420 Sikhs ('Australian Sikhs Census 2016', 2016). However, numbers have likely increased since 2016, given recent migration trends from India and especially from the Punjab. Having stated that, it is safe to surmise that the Sikh population on the Gold Coast is not as large as in Greater Melbourne, which has 39% of Australia's Sikh population; Greater Sydney, with 21%; or Greater Brisbane, where 10% of Sikh Australians have settled ('Sikhism in Australia', n.d.). Despite their limited numbers, Gold Coast Sikhs have inserted themselves successfully and productively into the framework of the local society and have contributed to the greater good through their constructive involvement in various fields, such as medicine, science, art, business, education and the service industries.

2.10 Gurdwaras: Woolgoolga, Murwillumbah, Brisbane and the Gold Coast

Before 2005, members of the Gold Coast Sikh community had no Gurdwara facilities of their own and, therefore, had to travel by road to Woolgoolga, Murwillumbah or Brisbane to pray. It was only from that year onwards that steps started being taken to conduct organised prayer assemblies on the Gold Coast, leading to the eventual establishment of two Sikh places of worship.

2.10.1 Woolgoolga

The presence of Sikhs in sufficiently large numbers generally results in the establishment of a Gurdwara, and Woolgoolga is a good example of this occurrence. By the 1940s, it had a noticeable Sikh population from the Punjab in India, made up largely of male banana-plantation workers who were hired to fill gaps left by white Australian workers who had joined the armed forces to fight in World War II.

As the years went by, the Sikh population grew, buoyed by a gradually increasing number of immigrants, especially from India. Many of them were family members of Sikh Punjabi males who had originally arrived alone. The steadily growing population maintained its strong ties to the Sikh faith and weekly prayer ceremonies were held at different homes or locations.

As the years passed, the community started seeing the value of having an established place where they could pray and meditate together but it was not until 1969 that a Gurdwara, the Guru Nanak Sikh Temple, was constructed, becoming the first purpose-built Gurdwara in Australia. Since then, many Gurdwaras have sprung up all over the country, which is testimony to the burgeoning Sikh population in Australia. This is in stark contrast to when just a few Sikhs arrived virtually unnoticed and unheralded more than a hundred and fifty years ago. The descendants of these trailblazers have gone on to own 95% of the banana industry in Woolgoolga and become '... solicitors, teachers, doctors, engineers, town planners, accountants and policemen' (More and Singh, n.d.).

2.10.2 Murwillumbah

Murwillumbah in New South Wales sits between the Gold Coast and Woolgoolga and has been home to Sikh families for many years, dating back to 1900. By the 1960s, the number of Sikh families in northern New South Wales had increased, especially around the Murwillumbah-Tweed and Mullumbimby-Bangalow regions. This increase was mainly due to the availability of jobs in the banana and sugarcane sectors. Murwillumbah became a popular spot for socialising on Friday evenings and it was not long before the concept of establishing a Gurdwara began to take shape.

To cater for their spiritual and community needs, a property on Nullum Street – in a picturesque part of town near the Tweed River – was rented in 1980 for Sikh prayers and meditation. This property was eventually bought with funds raised through donations, and in 1983 it was converted into a Gurdwara. The Gurdwara served the Sikhs well for fifteen years and attracted not only local congregants but also many from the Gold Coast, Brisbane, Lismore, Mullumbimby, Bangalow, Tweed, Numinbah Valley and Coffs Harbour.

With the number of attendees growing from year to year, it became necessary to expand and it was not long before the Sikh community purchased an adjoining property, again with donations raised by the Gurdwara Committee. These donations came from various donors, including non-Sikhs, from as far away as the Sunshine Coast, Toowoomba, Brisbane, the Gold Coast and other places. Work began in 1999 on the construction of a purpose-built Gurdwara, and in 2000 the Murwillumbah Sikh Temple opened its doors to a large assembly. The building that had been used as a Gurdwara since 1993 became a *langgar* hall. In 2004, an adjoining block of land was purchased and converted into a car park.

During the Covid-19 pandemic in 2020, the Murwillumbah Sikh Temple premises became the focal point for those adversely affected by the ensuing lockdown. Free vegetarian takeaway meals were provided for international students and other persons in need – a humanitarian gesture replicated by other Gurdwaras around the country. Cash donations and food kits from a variety of sources, including congregants, Khalsa Aid, and Turbans 4 Australia, helped the Sikh Temple provide cooked meals that could be picked up at the Gurdwara between 6.30 pm and 8.30 pm every day. Though the crisis has abated somewhat, this act of goodwill continues at the Gurdwara. The stellar work done by Ranbir Singh Bhorla (the secretary of the Murwillumbah Sikh Temple) and Surjit Singh Dhillon deserves special acknowledgement. Surjit took on the responsibility of providing cooked meals, while Ranbir helped serve and deliver them, which, in turn, helped raise the profile of the Murwillumbah Sikh Temple.

2.10.3 Brisbane

Sikhs have been a part of the Brisbane population for more than 50 years ('History of Brisbane Sikh Temple', n.d.), with the earliest record of the presence of Sikhs in Brisbane being registered in 1844 (Kenna and Jordan, 2015b). The first official Gurdwara in Brisbane, the Brisbane Sikh Temple, was opened in December 1988 at 2679 Logan Road. Prior to its opening, religious ceremonies involving local Sikhs were initially (in 1981) conducted in rented premises at Camp Hill School of Arts and later, from 1982 until 1988, in a hall rented from the Welfare Association for the Blind in Wooloongabba.

Major renovations have taken place since the establishment of the Brisbane Sikh Temple to cater for the increasing number of Sikh visitors from Brisbane and farther afield. The ever-growing Sikh population has led to three more Sikh temples being established in Brisbane: the Guru Nanak Sikh Temple at 16 Rosemary Street, Inala; the Singh Sabha Brisbane Gurdwara at 101 Lemke Road, Taigum; and the Khalsa-Kaumi-Shaheedan Gurdwara Sahib in Mackenzie.

2.10.4 Gold Coast

Until 2005, there was no formal building on the Gold Coast that represented a Gurdwara, and religious gatherings were held privately in homes. Gold Coasters wishing to pray in a proper Gurdwara had no option other than to drive north to Brisbane or south to Murwillumbah or Woolgoolga. As not all families wished to travel these distances, discussions soon started on how the community could go about establishing a local Gurdwara.

The first meaningful steps were taken on 11 June 2005, when Gold Coast Sikhs got together in rented premises at the Robina Community Centre to conduct the inaugural community-wide, Gurdwara-based, local prayer and meditation ceremony. This historic step was largely due to the initiative of Professor Bee Chen Goh, also known as Tej Kaur, originally from Malaysia and a Gold Coast resident since 1991. Meditation and prayer assemblies were held regularly from that point onwards, ranging from fortnightly to monthly.

Things progressed smoothly and the congregation grew as more and more Sikhs became aware of the existence of religious services on the Gold Coast. Before long, it was felt that the gradually expanding Sikh community would benefit from being part of an official umbrella organisation to represent them on specific matters pertaining to their welfare and interests. A formal application was made to the Office of Fair Trading, Queensland. The application proved to be successful and, before long, led to the formation of the Gold Coast Sikh Association Incorporated in 2010.

For the next eight years, the association continued conducting assemblies in rented premises in Robina and Nerang with an eye on possessing its own permanent property at some point. Various urban and rural premises were inspected over the next few years, none of which proved to be suitable. Eventually, in 2018, the Gold Coast Sikh Association purchased a large, established building at 5 Palings Court, Nerang, and successfully converted it into a Gurdwara with the Gold Coast City Council's approval.

This place of worship was named the Gurdwara Sahib Gold Coast and on 1 January 2019, the first ever formal Sikh prayer gathering in a designated place of worship on the Gold Coast was organised by the Gold Coast Sikh Association. Shortly after this first assembly in recognised premises, another organisation, the Gold Coast Sikh Council – an initiative of Surjit Ahluwalia Singh – established its own purpose-built Gurdwara, the Guru Maneyo Granth Gurdwara in Helensvale, and conducted its first meditation and prayer assembly at its official opening on 11 April 2019.

3

Pre-1980 and 1980 to 2020: Some Gold Coast Sikh Personalities

Sing the songs of joy to the Lord,
Serve the Name of the Lord
And become the servant of his servants.

Guru Nanak Dev Ji

3.1 Pre-1980 Gold Coast

As indicated in Chapter 2, there appears to have been no concerted or focused attempt by the British-era Australian authorities to make detailed records of Sikhs living and working around Australia, including on the Gold Coast. However, there are some exceptions to this apparent lack of information.

The name Bob Singh is mentioned in records related to the Burleigh Bears Rugby League Football Club, which he founded in 1934, and the Bob Singh Oval in the Pizzey Park complex at 80 Pacific Avenue, Miami, which is also named after him. The likelihood that he was a Sikh is very strong, given that virtually all early migrants with that surname came from the Punjab, the Sikh homeland.

Another probable indicator of the presence of Sikhs on the Gold Coast in the early 1900s is the existence of a street in Tugun called Singh Street. There may have been enough Sikhs living in the vicinity, probably working as banana-plantation workers, sugar cane labourers or dairy farmhands in Currumbin Valley, to warrant the street name. In addition, because Coolangatta, which is located next to Tugun, exported thoroughbred horses to India (Coolangatta Estate, n.d.), it is possible that Sikhs were hired to look after the horses and lived together on Singh Street.

3.2 Gold Coast Sikhs – 1980 to 2020

The following section provides four decades worth of information on a cross-section of Gold Coast Sikh families and individuals who may be of interest to future generations of Gold Coasters from a historical perspective. As a matter of interest, mention is made of individual achievements that represent 'firsts' among Gold Coast Sikhs.

Going by anecdotal evidence, the presence of Sikhs on the Gold Coast only began to be widely acknowledged from the 1980s onwards. Since that time, various individuals have contributed, in one way or another, to raise the profile of Sikhs in the region.

The forthcoming sections describe some of them. The information is based on a combination of established facts, the author's recollection of events, assumptions made based on available information, and, predominately, personal communication (face-to-face interviews, telephone chats and online communication) with Gold Coast Sikh individuals. They were approached one by one and their permission was sought, directly or indirectly, before they were included.

As such, this record does not claim to represent absolute historical accuracy and the list is not exhaustive – there are likely other high-achieving Sikhs on the Gold Coast whose stories haven't been included, either because they have not been involved in Sikh community activities or because they are unknown to the author. Additionally, there were a few who did not respond to requests for interviews or information that could be included in the book, and some preferred not to participate in the project.

Details about the individuals in the coming pages vary in length from person to person, simply because some provided more information about themselves while others provided less. Participants were invited to proofread information about themselves at various stages during the writing of this book and encouraged to expand on information about their achievements and contributions to the community as much as possible. The results have been included where provided.

3.2.1 Kewal and Surjit Dhillon

The late Kewal Singh Dhillon was probably the first Gold Coast Sikh to gain a noticeable public profile in the 1980s, principally through his involvement in the Indian food business as a restaurateur. He could be said to have been the forerunner of all the Sikh-operated Indian restaurants currently operating on the Gold Coast, as there is no known record of any other Sikh involved in the Indian restaurant business prior to his venture.

Kewal, originally from India, first started out as a Gold Coast restaurateur by running an Indian restaurant called the Raja Mataj in collaboration with a partner. The restaurant commenced business at Centrepoint Surfers Paradise in 1980. Later, in 1983, he opened his own restaurant, Tandoori Taj, in Surfers Paradise. It was a grand opening – Kewal made an entrance on an elephant, Indian maharajah style, alongside six Rolls Royces. Kewal was joined by his brother from India, Surjit Singh Dhillon, on 9 January 1984. The brothers worked together to make their restaurant a very popular place for diners with a taste for Indian food.

Surjit eventually took over the running of the restaurant. He went on to operate Tandoori Place Indian Restaurant, the formal opening of which (in 2006) was as colourful as that of Tandoori Taj and included the presence of an elephant. He has remained a popular personality in the Indian food business on the Gold Coast, with his culinary skills very much in demand. Patrons who organise private events like birthdays or festival celebrations often turn to him for catering.

Surjit has also been an active foundation and committee member of the Gold Coast Sikh Association and has played an important role in the development of the Gurdwara Sahib Gold Coast in Nerang through donation-seeking activities, *langgar* preparations, sponsoring communal meals and making time to assist in renovations, as well as making equipment, monetary and food donations.

During the 2020 worldwide coronavirus pandemic, Surjit demonstrated his generosity and goodwill by participating in a singularly charitable endeavour. In collaboration with the Gurdwara Sahib Gold Coast and the Murwillumbah Sikh Temple, he was one of a core group of individuals who initiated a free food project. The undertaking provided a meals-pickup service from his restaurant and the Nerang and Murwillumbah Gurdwaras, to Gold Coast and Murwillumbah lockdown victims facing financial hardships or suffering food shortage, at no cost to them.

Surjit not only did extensive cooking himself but also gave volunteers open access to his kitchen to allow them to prepare meals for distribution to those who needed it most. Frontline workers in the University Hospital Gold Coast and Robina Hospital were among those who benefitted from this *seva*, with many sending messages of thanks on public online platforms. He also personally helped deliver food to the hospitals, together with the Gold Coast Sikh Association, Khalsa Aid Australia, Turbans 4 Australia and Australia India Club. In these unstinting humanitarian deeds, Surjit was enthusiastically assisted by Ranbir Singh Bhorla, who was ever ready to lend a helping hand when required.

3.2.2 The Samra Family

Another Gold Coast Sikh family of note is the Samra family, whose antecedents are mentioned in Chapter 2 (Section 2.7). Rashpaul Singh Samra, who had worked in the United Kingdom as an engineer for British Gas, arrived in Australia in 1980 with his wife, Rajwans Kaur Samra (they are often referred to as Paul and Rose by locals), and their three children, Pam, Pauline and Jeff. The family's initial plan had been to make Cairns their home but they found the climate unsuitable and moved to Sydney. Shortly after that, they came to the Gold Coast and decided to make it their permanent place of residence.

Between 1980 and 1992, Paul and Rose purchased and developed four newsagencies in Palm Beach, Burleigh Heads and Burleigh. They also purchased a childcare centre in Ashmore in 1987 (to ensure that their daughter, Danielle, would have a childcare place), and a loans office in Surfers Paradise. In addition, they ventured into hydroponics farming in Woolgoolga, New South Wales, in 1996, and their farm became an integral part of the local Technical and Further Education (TAFE) academic curriculum. Always one to expand his horizons, Paul recently purchased the iconic Pacific Avenue Markets in Miami.

Since his retirement, Paul has been working as a volunteer for the Meals on Wheels programme and has also helped the Never Alone organisation plan and carry out trips and social gatherings for the elderly. He exemplifies the Australian spirit of caring and sharing, a spirit that is also abundantly evident in Sikhism.

Paul and Rose see themselves as assimilated Australians and have passed on this sense of belonging to their children. Their five grandsons – Connor, Yuvraj, Jaye, Quin, and Ishan – are beneficiaries of their belief in the value of being part of the local culture.

Rashpaul and Rajwan's eldest daughter, Pamela, is an occupational therapist who graduated with honours from the University of Queensland. She also has a Bachelor of Psychological Science (Honours) degree, which she secured from Central Queensland University in 2017. Pamela's expertise in occupational therapy has led to her being appointed as a lecturer in psychiatry to occupational therapy and medical students at Bond University in the Faculty of Health Sciences and Medicine. Furthermore, she has participated in ground-breaking research on occupational therapy for mental health and older adults, resulting in the publication of various articles in peer-reviewed journals like the *British Journal of Therapy and Rehabilitation*, the *British Journal of Occupational Therapy* and the *Journal of Ageing and Physical Activity*.

As a schoolchild, Pamela sang in her school's choir at a national-level competition held at the Sydney Opera House, the first Gold Coast Sikh child to do so.

At present, she and her husband, Dr Ashok Chauhan, operate several medical centres. Ashok is also the brains behind the Indian Gold Coast

Community, set up in February 2017 to help Gold Coast Indians link up with each other. In 2018, Ashok and his colleague, Amrit Bhorla, started an informal group designed to promote connections through monthly social gatherings for Gold Coast Indians over the age of sixty-five. Both Ashok and Pamela have organised large-scale Indian cultural events like Diwali nights and Holi festivals.

Paul and Rose's second child, Pauline Samra, is a practising lawyer and plays a prominent role in public service by liaising with bureaucrats in Canberra. Pauline graduated from the University of Queensland with a Science degree and then went on to complete a Bachelor of Laws at Bond University in 1994.

Jeff Samra, the third child in the family, was the first Sikh graduate of Bond University, completing his Bachelor of Commerce degree in December 1991. He is married to Anu Samra, who has achieved a couple of firsts among Gold Coast Sikhs. She was the 2017/2018 Mrs Punjaban Australia, a title awarded to the most outstanding married woman of Punjabi descent, based on her intellect and knowledge of Sikh culture and philosophies, among other things. Prior to that, she had won the Mrs Punjaban Queensland. Jeff and Anu oversee the operation of the Pacific Avenue Markets and run childcare businesses. They are keen supporters of the Havafeed organisation, which caters for the needs of the homeless and the disenfranchised.

The youngest child, Dr Danielle Williams née Samra, is married to Dr Zoheb Williams, a vascular surgeon at Gold Coast University Hospital. Danielle and her husband practised medicine in Newcastle, Brisbane, Townsville and New Zealand, before returning to the Gold Coast. She now works with Ashok as a General Practitioner in the family medical practice.

3.2.3 The Ahluwalia Family

Shortly after the Dhillon brothers and Samra family had established themselves on the Gold Coast, there was a steady stream of new Sikh arrivals. Dr Jagat Jit Ahluwalia Singh was one of them. He arrived in 1987 with his wife, Kamaljit Kaur, and two young children, Kuljit and Surjit. He was the Gold Coast's first Sikh doctor and ran a successful practice in Mermaid, eventually moving it to Coolangatta. Jagat Jit and Kamaljit have five grandchildren.

Jagat Jit was a foundation member and committee member of the Gold Coast Sikh Association and played a significant role in conducting prayers at the very first Sikh prayer assembly at the Robina Community Centre in 2005. He served as president of the association from 2013 to 2014 and provided various services to the Sikh community in the form of leading prayer ceremonies and participating in *kirtan* singing.

Jagat Jit's home has been the focal point for Sikhs from the Gold Coast, Brisbane and Murwillumbah to gather for social and meditation gatherings since 1988, with Jagat Jit and Kamaljit as hosts. There is a very high probability that his family was the first on the Gold Coast to have their own copy of the Guru Granth Sahib Ji.

In 2017, Jagat Jit became one of three directors of the newly formed Gold Coast Sikh Council that was established to lay the foundation for the Gold Coast's first purpose-built Gurdwara, which was approved by the Gold Coast City Council – the Guru Maneyo Granth Gurdwara in Helensvale.

Jagat Jit is a committed Sikh who dedicates a significant portion of his time to furthering Sikh principles and philosophies among Gold Coast Sikhs. As a respected and knowledgeable Sikh elder, he is often approached by members of the community to lead prayer ceremonies at religious functions.

Jagat Jit and Kamaljit Kaur's daughter, Kuljit, arrived on the Gold Coast with her family when she was 11 and was the first Sikh schoolgirl at the prestigious St Hilda School in Southport. After completing high school, she studied medicine at the University of Tasmania and graduated with a medical degree with honours. She followed in her father's footsteps and entered general practice at the age of 26. She was Associate Professor of General Practice at Bond University, Gold Coast, in the university's 2004 to 2005 sessions.

Besides being a medical practitioner, Kuljit has a keen interest in the arts, particularly music, singing and dancing. Among her achievements are singing vocals on her first album, 'Antrik Aatma' by Shaia, in 2007. Kuljit's song 'Mun na digay' won a song-writing award in Sydney and was also bought by Samsara Lounge, making her the first Gold Coast Sikh to achieve this distinction. Before releasing the album, she had recorded three songs with Chartsong Production Brisbane.

Together with her brother, Surjit, Kuljit organised a variety of Indian community and cultural events through Bollywood Fusion, which they established to cater to the social needs of the Indian Community and to advance Indian culture within the wider community. She has also used her music and dance talents to foster interest about Indian culture in young children.

Among her other Gold Coast Sikh firsts, Kuljit was one of the contestants in the 2002 Miss India Worldwide competition held in Durban, South Africa; she played a cameo role in a Bollywood movie filmed on the Gold Coast; and she was a radio presenter on the community radio station, 4EB.

In addition to her contributions to the performing arts, Kuljit has participated in *kirtan* singing at the Gold Coast, Brisbane and Murwillumbah Gurdwara assemblies and has also played an active part in organising and participating in fundraising events like the Gold Coast Sikh Association dinner-and-dance evenings.

Kuljit and her husband, Maninderjit Singh Kala (see Chapter 3.2.28), co-founded a not-for-profit health voluntary initiative called Our Health Vikas to advocate preventative health medicine and community well-being on the Gold Coast. Maninderjit initiated this project and he and Kuljit received valuable assistance from Dr Sonu Haikerwal and her husband, Raj Haikerwal. The project was established under the auspices of the Gold Coast Sikh Council and the Guru Maneyo Granth Gurdwara in Helensvale. Our Health Vikas has proved to be a very popular resource for those requiring assistance.

Kuljit and Maninderjit have two little daughters, Anishka, who is seven, and Jiya, who is four. Anishka and Jiya participated in a Kids4Kids YouTube video titled 'Mr Corona' to raise awareness among young children about Covid-19 and the steps they can take to avoid the effects of coronavirus. In the process, they became the first Sikh children not only on the Gold Coast but in the whole of Australia to appear in a public platform video of this nature.

Born in Bendigo in 1980, Surjit, the son of Jagat Jit and Kamaljit, has worn his Sikh identity with pride at all levels – social, physical and corporate. He was the first turbaned and practising Sikh schoolboy to study at The Southport School (TSS) and, quite probably, on the Gold Coast. At school, Surjit was commended for his academic and sporting prowess. He played school cricket, as well as club (Broadbeach United) and school soccer, all the while maintaining his Sikh identity.

Although he completed his schooling in Melbourne, Surjit has always been a Gold Coaster at heart. He returned to the Gold Coast for his tertiary studies at Bond University, where he successfully completed his undergraduate studies in accounting and met his wife-to-be Czarina, the Gold Coast's first Sikh of caucasian descent.

At University, Surjit filled a void for many students by organising Indian Cultural Nights and was also a local disc jockey from 1999 to 2007. He was very keen to bring Indian culture to the Gold Coast and so, together with his sister Kuljit and wife Czarina, he established the first local Indian entertainment business, formally known as Bollywood Fusion.

After completing his degree, Surjit worked as a business advisor in public practice, later moving into commerce and acquiring CPA, ACMA and CIMA qualifications. His business acumen and dedication allowed him to climb the corporate ladder, achieving the position of Financial Controller for the Worldmark Group at the young age of twenty-four. Surjit's drive saw him hold other significant executive positions in multinational companies, open large hotels, and manage large teams across the country – again a Gold Coast first for a practising Sikh who wore his turban and beard with distinction.

Surjit has used his entrepreneurial skills to establish his own successful business that provides various property services. Furthermore, his business has been able to sponsor the Magic United Soccer Club on the Gold Coast, with his company logo displayed on the players' jerseys, also a Gold Coast first for a successful Sikh-operated business.

A keen sportsman, Surjit organised and trained the first-ever Gold Coast Sikh Soccer teams for men and ladies – the Gold Coast Sikharoos – which took part in the Melbourne Australian Sikh Games in April 2007.

Always willing to lend a hand, Surjit was an active member of the Gold Coast Sikh Association in its early days, assisting with congregations and playing the tabla as needed.

Over time, he saw the need for a formal, purpose-built Gurdwara that would allow Sikh philosophies to be practised unencumbered, in a religious establishment open seven days a week. Using his community-leadership expertise, he personally sought consent from the Gold Coast City Council and was given approval to proceed on 10 April 2017. Subsequently, the Gold

Coast's very first *Nee Patthhar di Rasam* (ground-breaking ceremony) for a Gurdwara was conducted on 7 October 2017 by *Punj Pyare* (Five Beloved Ones): Dr Jagat Jit Ahluwalia Singh, Jagdish (Gajan) Hayer, Bhajan Singh Bains, Beant Singh and Teja Singh.

Construction work commenced after this historical event and, on 11 April 2019, the first purpose-built Gurdwara and Community Education Centre on the Gold Coast, the Guru Maneyo Granth Gold Coast Gurdwara, was officially opened in Helensvale after a *Nagar Kirtan* (holy hymns sung by local congregants). The Guru Maneyo Granth Gold Coast Gurdwara is open seven days a week and provides *langgar* to its congregants. It has its own resident *Raagi Jattha* (hymn-singers) who conduct prayers, sermons and marriages.

Surjit is also the founder and general manager of the Gold Coast Sikh Council (a registered Australian charity), which operates the Guru Maneyo Granth Gold Coast Gurdwara at 9–11 Shepparton Road, Helensvale. The council has over 3,500 Facebook followers at the time of writing.

Surjit was one of two Sikhs who made Gold Coast history by being the first Sikhs selected to hold the Queen's Baton during the opening relay of the Commonwealth Games on the Gold Coast in 2018. The other Sikh was Mokhtiar Singh of the Gold Coast Sikh Association.

Surjit's children have followed in the path of their father's lifestyle by being devout Sikhs who participate in community activities. His eldest child, Devraj Singh, plays club basketball. His second son, Sartaj Singh, is an avid soccer player who has been selected to train with the Gold Coast Premier League Squad at the young age of nine. The youngest in the family, Munleen Kaur, is also into soccer. The boys play the harmonium and tabla and sing *shabad* (hymns) at the Guru Maneyo Granth Gold Coast Gurdwara, accompanied by their younger sister and cousins.

3.2.4 Mokhtiar Singh

Another prominent Gold Coast Sikh, Mokhtiar Singh, moved from Malaysia to the Gold Coast in 1988. He held various positions before opting to join the police force in 1993. In the process, he created history by becoming Queensland's, and Australia's, first orthodox Sikh to be sworn in as a police officer in Queensland. The most significant outcome of this event was that it led to an important change to the uniform of Queensland police officers. Prior to his appointment, turbans had never formed part of the uniform. It was only after consultation with London Metropolitan Police and Malaysian authorities regarding the wearing of turbans by their police officers that approval was given for the turban to be included in the Queensland police service. Since Mokhtiar's appointment, Australia has witnessed an increasing number of turbaned Sikh police officers in various states, a testimony to his trailblazing legacy.

Mokhtiar retired in 2014 and currently works for a non-profit organisation called The Migrant Centre as a principal training and employment officer and is also in legal solutions.

Among his other achievements, Mok, as he is popularly known, is the first Sikh in the Varsity Lakes Rotary Club, the first Sikh to hold the office of Secretary of the International Police Association, Queensland branch, and the first Sikh to hold the office of Vice-President of the Australian Computer Society, Gold Coast branch. He is also an Alumni Ordinary Member of Bond University Limited and the Gold Coast Alumni Chapter, having graduated from Bond with a Master of Laws degree.

In 2018, Mokhtiar (together with Surjit Ahluwalia Singh of the Gold Coast Sikh Council) was selected to participate in the Queen's Baton Relay for the Gold Coast Commonwealth Games. This event was historic because Gold Coast Sikhs had never previously participated in such an important prelude to an international sporting event of this magnitude.

Mokhtiar is a foundation and committee member of the Gold Coast Sikh Association and has served as the official secretary of the association since 2011 (except during his term of presidency). His main role as secretary is to oversee the smooth day-to-day running of the Gurdwara. He was also the president of the association for two consecutive terms, from 2015 to 2017.

Mokhtiar has been of significant assistance to the association through sponsoring *langgar*, participating in fundraising drives, ensuring that Gurdwara assemblies are run efficiently and securing government grants for the association's projects and activities. Specifically, he obtained two Federal Government grants for computers, electronic devices and kitchen appliances, one grant from the Gold Coast City Council for Seniors' Week, one each from the Queensland Attorney General's Department and Multicultural Queensland for cultural events and one each from the Federal and State Governments for kitchen refurbishment. In addition, Mokhtiar identified funds that led to the installation of solar panels at the Gurdwara. Financial lifelines like these have enabled the Gurdwara Sahib Gold Coast to cater to the needs of its congregants competently.

As a further indication of his dedication to the Gold Coast Sikh Association, he was one of the active volunteers who helped physically during renovations to the Gurdwara in the early days, soon after its acquisition.

During the Covid-19 pandemic and subsequent lockdown, Mokhtiar played a crucial role in being of assistance and supplying food to struggling international students from various parts of the world. He also took on the task of delivering savoury snacks, pickles and *masala chai* (spice tea) to Australians returning from India who were quarantined at the Voco Hotel in Surfers Paradise at the height of the pandemic in May 2020. This was done with the assistance and support of Police Liaison Officer Sam Narayan of the Queensland Police Service.

Mokhtiar's wife, Adeline Yap-Singh, is the Principal Solicitor of AH Lawyers located in Southport. She is a founding member of the Robina Community Legal Centre (RCLC), which provides free legal assistance to Gold Coasters in need.

3.2.5 Balwinder Singh Reehal

Another Sikh to leave his mark on the Gold Coast was Balwinder Singh Reehal, or 'Bob' as he came to be known by the locals. He came to the Gold Coast in 1988 after spending more than six years in Sydney where he worked for Ultra Tune as a troubleshooting mechanic. Shortly after his arrival, he purchased the Ultra Tune outlet in Southport, becoming the first Gold Coast Sikh to purchase and own that franchise. Over the years, Balwinder became quite well known in the car-repair industry, with a wide range of clients from both the Indian and non-Indian communities.

He also found time for spiritual meditation and was deeply involved in the practice of character-plus mental and moral development through good citizenship. Balwinder has been a Freemason for twenty-eight years and has been a Worshipful Master three times at the Broadwater Surfers Paradise Lodge in Southport. He is currently serving a second term as Worshipful Master at Maroochydore Lodge, Sunshine Coast. In addition, Balwinder is a member of the Masonic Royal Arch Chapter and the Secret Monitor.

Balwinder has three daughters, twins Jade Kaur and Jasier Kaur, and India Kaur Reehal. Jade teaches in Coolum Secondary School and is the Head of Department of Physical Education. She is a taekwondo exponent, having achieved fifth-dan black-belt status. Her achievements include being a state champion and representing Australia in taekwondo at the Open Championship in Korea in 1999, the first Gold Coast Sikh to do so.

Jade's sister, Jasier, is also a taekwondo enthusiast and owner of a fourth-dan black belt. She was a state and national champion at the under-14 level in 2002. Jasier is a state-registered nurse and is currently stationed at Southampton Hospital in England on a three-year work visa.

India, the youngest of the three sisters, also has a black belt in taekwondo. Besides the martial arts, as an athlete she has won silver medals in the 400 metres and 800 metres and a bronze in the 1500 metres at a state-level athletic event. India is a senior technician nurse at Carrara Vet on the Gold Coast.

Balwinder moved to the Sunshine Coast in 2016, where he currently lives with his wife, Hae Young Jung.

Young Jung is a South Korean of the Christian faith but that does not stop her from having a broad-minded affinity for Sikhism. She has researched the ethics associated with Sikhism and makes it a point to visit Gurdwaras whenever she can.

3.2.6 Inder Singh Jaswal

The next high-profile Sikh to reach the Gold Coast was Inder Singh Jaswal. Inder moved from Melbourne to the Gold Coast in 1989 with plans to start an Indian restaurant. After studying the market and considering various options, he opened House of India in Nerang in 1990. The growing popularity of Indian cuisine led him to consider fresh options and he eventually opened another House of India, this time in Broadbeach Mall. Later, Inder established The Indian and Agnee in Robina. He still owns and runs Agnee, which is very popular among Indian-food enthusiasts.

In 1998, Inder became the first Gold Coast Sikh restaurateur to win the Restaurant and Caterers Award, an across-the-board award that covered all ethnic restaurants, not just Indian ones.

Over the years, he has unflinchingly helped some of his staff start their own restaurants, thereby increasing the number of successful Indian food outlets on the Gold Coast. A forthright man with a big heart, Inder has played foster-parent to international students who worked for him, providing accommodation and meals and helping pay for their education. He has also donated his money and time to the religious and social activities of Gold Coast Sikhs.

Inder married Janice McDougal on 18 March 1978. They have two children, Arjun and Sonia.

While in Melbourne, he earned the distinction of being the first turbaned taxi-driver and the first motorcyclist to be exempted by the authorities from wearing a crash-helmet because of his turban.

He was also a keen sportsman in his younger years and was involved with local clubs in cricket, hockey and archery. Inder eventually became a motorcycle aficionado and is the first Sikh motorcycle enthusiast on the Gold Coast. He currently owns a Suzuki Boulevard that he uses as his occasional means of transport to work, but which he rides mostly for recreational purposes.

3.2.7 The Ahlavadi Family

Amarjeet Singh Ahlavadi (or Micky, as he is popularly known to the locals), and his wife, Vimmi, both bachelor-degree holders, arrived on the Gold Coast in 1989, together with their children, Arjun and Vrinda. Amarjeet first ventured into the food business in 1995 by starting an Indian restaurant in Chevron called Curry Muncher. In 1998 he opened another restaurant, Delhi Darbar, in Surfers Paradise, which he still operates. Amarjeet and Vimmi take pride in their culinary offerings, and their dedication to giving the best possible service to their customers has made Delhi Darbar very popular with locals and overseas visitors. Delhi Darbar also supplied food free of charge for fundraising events like Desi Night, which used to be a major Gold Coast Indian community event.

Amarjeet is not just a businessman but also a popular social figure who is well-liked by those who know him because of his calm and gentle nature, his kindness and his ever-present smile. As a foundation member and committee member of the Gold Coast Sikh Association, he has played a crucial role in helping to raise funds for the association. He and Vimmi unfailingly exhibit the Sikh principle of service to others by contributing to *langgar seva* (service associated with the provision of free vegetarian meals) on numerous occasions. In addition, he has supplied the Nerang Gurdwara Sahib Gold Coast with assistance in securing major equipment central to the functioning of meditation services, including television monitors to stream Sikh religious events.

During the Covid-19 pandemic, Amarjeet served the community generously by taking part in the preparation and distribution of free vegetarian meals to those who had become victims of the subsequent lockdown. His restaurant was one of the focal points for the preparation and cooking of these meals by volunteers, who were given free access to his kitchen.

Amarjeet and Vimi's son, Arjun Ahlavadi, completed his Bachelor of Business and Events at Griffith University and is currently pursuing further studies in audio engineering.

Their daughter, Vrinda Ahlavadi, was the first Sikh child to be accepted into the Queensland Academy of Technology. She completed a Bachelor of Dietetics and Nutrition at Griffith University and is currently on placement at Cairns Hospital. Vrinda is also a gifted performing artist, particularly as a dancer, and has lent her talents to fundraising events for the Gold Coast Sikh Association.

3.2.8 The CS Gill Family

Chamkaur Singh Gill and his wife, Professor Bee Chen Goh, who took the Sikh name Tej Kaur after her *Amrit Sanchar* ceremony, left Malaysia for the Gold Coast in 1991. Bee Chen is the first Sikh of Chinese ancestry on the Gold Coast. She is also the first Gold Coast Sikh to take up an academic position in the Faculty of Law at Bond University, Australia's premier private university.

In 2006, Bee Chen joined Southern Cross University and became its inaugural female Head of the School of Law and Justice; her decanal appointment in the discipline of law was, notably, another Sikh first in Australia. She remains, at present, a professor of law at this university. Her various achievements include being the first Malaysian female Rhodes Scholar, fellow and director of the pre-eminent Australian Academy of Law and chair of the academy's Prizes and Scholarships Committee, fellow of the Cambridge Commonwealth Society, and fellow of the Society for Advanced Legal Studies in London. She served on the Queensland Rhodes Scholarship Selection Committee from 2011 to 2014. Bee Chen has also held visiting academic roles at Harvard Law School, the Institute of Advanced Legal Studies at the University of London, the Faculty of Law at Bergen University in Norway and the Faculty of Law at Chiang Mai University in Thailand.

Bee Chen is a well-published author of books, journal articles and conference papers, particularly in dispute resolution with a focus on Sino-Western issues, and international law of peace (including law and religion on inter-faith matters). Notably, she was invited to present at a forum with His Holiness the Dalai Lama XIV at Monash University in 2007 during His Holiness' Australian Tour. Some of her research is used as reference material in international universities and colleges. Her other scholarly interests include climate justice and organics, and law and theatre. Bee Chen will soon embark on the Shakespeare Moot Project for the School of Law and Justice, at Southern Cross University.

Dating back to 2005, Bee Chen was one of the initial driving forces behind the progression of the Gold Coast Sikh community's religious and communal activities, with regular gatherings organised by the initial foundational members at the Robina Community Centre. Her enterprise flowed over to the formation of the Gold Coast Sikh Association in 2010, which, in turn, led to the establishment of a place of worship at 5 Palings Court, Nerang in 2018. Bee Chen has played an important role in the Gold Coast Sikh Association's initial fundraising initiatives through securing donations and participating in community events.

Chamkaur joined Bond University to teach English, literature, drama and applied linguistics in the Faculty of Humanities and Social Sciences (now renamed the Faculty of Society and Design), thereby becoming the first Sikh to do so. He won the Bond University inaugural Award for Excellence in Learning and Teaching of International Students in 2009.

Prior to that, his teaching methodology was one of 44 (from an original list of 2000 respondents) selected in 1997 for entry into a publication by the Committee for University Teaching and Staff Development. In the same year, Bond University nominated him for the Australian Awards (Institutional) for University Teaching and, in 1998, he was invited to be an advisor on applications for the 1999 National Teaching Development Grants.

As a researcher, Chamkaur has had various academic articles published in international journals and his work has been cited by academic researchers worldwide. In 2015, he was selected as a reviewer for the *Bilingual Research Journal*, a Routledge publication. Currently, he is on the editorial panel of an online journal, *Advances in Language and Literary Studies.*

Chamkaur retired from Bond University at the beginning of 2018, after forty-five years of teaching (in Malaysia and Australia) and now spends time on literary pursuits, writing books, poetry and plays. During his time at Bond University, he staged numerous theatrical productions and is currently a drama consultant and play director for a local theatre company, Wild Dreamer Productions. A play he wrote recently titled *Void*, scheduled for staging under his directorship in March 2020, had to be indefinitely postponed when the global pandemic hit. He also wrote the lyrics for the songs in the play, which deals with issues linked to child abduction.

Chamkaur served as president of the Gold Coast Sikh Association from

2014 to 2015. During his days as committee member of the association, he helped raise funds by organising cultural events like Desi Night and securing donations from individuals and organisations in Australia and Malaysia. In the Gold Coast Sikh Association's pre-incorporation foundational years, Chamkaur acted as the ad hoc secretary from 2005 until the association's formal incorporation in 2010, relinquishing this role in early 2011.

Mindy Kaur Gill, Chamkaur and Bee Chen's daughter, is an award-winning writer and poet whose poems have been published in various literary magazines in Australia and overseas. She graduated from the Queensland University of Technology with First Class Honours in Poetry.

Mindy had her first poem published when she was an eight-year-old in primary school. Among her accolades, Mindy has been awarded the Queensland Premier's Young Writers and Publishers Award, the Tom Collins Poetry Prize, a Wheeler Centre Hot Desk Fellowship, residencies with Sangam House in Bangalore, the Chennai Mathematical Institute Arts Initiative Residency in partnership with Sangam House, the Melbourne Visiting Poets Programme, the 2020 Swatch Art Peace Hotel Artist Residency in Shanghai, and is the winner of the 2020 *Australian Poetry* Nature, Art and Habitat Residency (*AP*/NAHR) Eco-Poetry Fellowship (conferred on a single Australian poet annually) in Sottochiesa, Tallegio Valley, northern Italy.

Mindy was part of the 2020 Australia Council delegation during the India Literature Exploratory in Jaipur and New Delhi. She has been a judge for the Queensland Literary Awards and is the current Editor-in-Chief of *Peril Magazine*, an online literary journal for Asian–Australian writing.

Mindy's other creative talents lie in art and pottery, which she learned from age 10. As a schoolchild, Mindy became the first Sikh to win first prize in a Gold Coast pottery competition for juniors. She also won other prizes and commendations at this Gold-Coast-run pottery competition over several years. Mindy graduated as the top student in art in her high school. When in school, her drawings and paintings were exhibited at the Mudgeeraba Show Ground (when she was in Year 2), and at the Gold Coast Arts Centre (now renamed Home of the Arts) when she was in Year 12.

3.2.9 The Calais Family

Malaysian-born Patwant Singh Calais, his wife, Balban Kaur Calais, and their family moved from Tasmania to the Gold Coast in 1991. Patwant, known to his friends and associates as Patty, was the first president of the Gold Coast Sikh Association Incorporated and held the position for two years (2010 to 2012). He is a foundation member of the association and has also served as a committee member.

During Patwant's term as president, Gurmukhi classes commenced on the Gold Coast – an important initiative for the community. Classes were conducted free of charge by Kamaljit Kaur and Ranjit Singh of the Guru Granth Sahib Ji Academy of Brisbane. Another notable achievement during his presidency was his aid in securing Deductible Gift Recipient (DGR) status for the Gold Coast Sikh Association. He also played an important role in helping draw up the association's constitution.

A lot of the success of the Gold Coast Sikh Association can be attributed to the assistance Patwant and his wife Balban Kaur Calais provided to community members involved in its activities, and to its acquisition, development and maintenance of the Nerang Gurdwara Sahib Gold Coast. Both have volunteered their services in the daily running of the Gurdwara and ensured the smooth conducting of regular assemblies, with Balban participating in hymn-singing from time to time. They have also involved themselves actively in Gold Coast community events, including contributing free meals to the homeless (with the support of Set Free Care).

Patwant helped raise a substantial sum of money for the Gold Coast Sikh Association through donations and fundraising. One such fundraising project was Desi Night, the first of which was held when he was president. His tireless efforts, in collaboration with other members of the association, played an important part in selling tickets and securing auction and raffle prizes, culminating in a very successful Desi Night. The event also paved the way for future events of a similar nature, resulting in a significant improvement to the funds of the Gold Coast Sikh Association.

Patwant holds a degree in agriculture and, as another of his achievements, he was the first Sikh to own and run a nursery on the Gold Coast, at the foothills of Mount Tamborine. Subsequently, since 2016, he has been the owner and operator of a blueberry farm in Grafton, New South Wales.

Their first son, Amolakh Singh Calais, attended The Southport School (TSS) from 1992 until he graduated in 1998. During his time at TSS, he was an avid sportsman and represented his school at cricket, soccer, tennis and rowing. He was a member of the first IV and the second VIII rowing squad. In his final year at TSS, Amolakh and his squad won the annual Great Public Schools' Association of Queensland (GPS) Head of the River Regatta.

During his time at TSS, he was selected by the staff and student populace to represent the school as its warden. This was a highly respectable position to hold and Amolakh performed his responsibilities with pride and honour. He was also a member of the TSS Navy Reserve Cadets for four years, eventually achieving the rank of Leading Seaman and Second-in-Charge of the Naval Reserve Cadet Unit.

Amolakh went on to do his tertiary studies at Bond University on the Gold Coast, graduating in 2002 with a double degree in commerce and information technology. After holding several senior positions with Microsoft in Sydney, he moved to Singapore to lead IBM's Regional Mid-Market Software business. He is currently the regional director of Asia-Pacific and Japan at TripAdvisor.

Amolakh is married to Paminderdip Kaur and they have three sons, Aaryan, Arjyan and Angayd. Parminderdip graduated from Edith Cowan University in Western Australia with a Bachelor of Accounting and E-Commerce in 2002. After working at the Australian Bureau of Statistics in Canberra, the Office of State Revenue and the Department of Treasury in Sydney, she decided to follow her passion for education and completed her master's degree in teaching. She is currently teaching at the Middleton International School in Singapore.

Gureaser Singh Calais, Patwant and Balban's younger son, was a corporal in the Air Force cadets at The Southport School. As the only turban-wearing Sikh in the corps, he was integral to changes to previously strict trainee uniform rules. A specially designed *patka* (head-cloth) was commissioned for him by an officer at the Amberley Airforce Base who was knowledgeable about Sikh turbans. Gureaser was given permission to wear it in place of the regular hats worn by trainees, thereby laying the groundwork for future Sikh students of The Southport School who wish to join the Air Force cadets.

Gureaser represented The Southport School as a delegate at the International Round Square Conference in Schleswig Holstein in Germany in 1999. He also competed at state level in kayaking, receiving a silver and a bronze medal at the Queensland Schoolboy Championships in 2000.

He graduated from Bond in 2004 with a Bachelor of Commerce (Marketing) degree. Following that, he went on to work in large national and multinational companies before deciding to make a career change and focus on service and health. He graduated from the Queensland University of Technology in 2013 with a Bachelor of Pharmacy.

Gureaser married Navjeet Kaur Randhawa in 2015 and they currently live in Melbourne. He manages a pharmacy in Thornbury, Melbourne, while Navjeet is a senior public servant with the Federal Government.

3.2.10 The Pasricha Family

Deepa Kaur Calais Pasricha (Deepa), the younger sister of Patwant Singh Calais and, like him, originally from Malaysia, first arrived on the Gold Coast in 1991 for postgraduate studies in law. She was the first Gold

Coast Sikh female law graduate from Bond University, completing her Master of Laws (Dispute Resolution and Arbitration) in 1993. Following the completion of her studies and after being called to the bar, she spent several years living and working in Melbourne, India and Malaysia. While in India, Deepa was very involved with the education of street children in Mumbai. In Malaysia, she invested a significant portion of time in supporting a Sikh children's home for orphans and children from difficult family backgrounds. Those connections are still a part of her commitments to charitable work.

Soon after returning to the Gold Coast in 2009 with her husband, Navin Pasricha, Deepa founded a media company based on a social enterprise model. According to Deepa, the company is dedicated to 'helping older Australians in their fifties and above, active retirees and seniors have a better life and to celebrate life. We provide practical and objective information on important areas of life, so that people can be aware of all the options they need to have a better quality of life'.

Deepa's publication, the *Australian Over 50s Living and Lifestyle Guidebook*, enjoys nationwide coverage and a readership of one million older Australians. She is often invited on television and radio to comment on issues affecting older generations in Australia. She has been recognised for her business acumen by being nominated for the Gold Coast's Businesswoman of the Year award.

Within the Sikh community, Deepa organised the very first *samelan* (Sikh youth camp) in Brisbane and, quite possibly, Queensland, in the mid-1990s. Her model for the *samelan* has served as an inspiration for many similar events since her pioneering work. She continues to be involved in *samelans* in Brisbane.

Deepa served as a committee member of the Gold Coast Sikh Association at various times between 2010 and 2018 and has played a major role in organising and participating in the association's fundraising community events like Desi Night and other health-related events.

Deepa is an active participant in the association's undertakings, contributing to social, educational and religious activities. She has been particularly active in initiatives to promote mental health and wellness in the community, and in the battle against domestic violence. She has organised talks on both these subjects for the Gurdwara community and has co-represented the Punjabi community in the government's efforts to fight domestic violence.

In addition to her voluntary community-related commitments, Deepa is a regular *kirtan* singer at the Nerang Gurdwara Sahib Gold Coast's weekly gatherings.

Deepa's husband, Navin Pasricha, whilst not born into Sikhism, comes from a Hindu family in which the *Gurbani* was recited daily and the three tenets of *Kirat Karo* (earn an honest living for the benefit of self, family and society), *Naam Japo* (Recite God's name) *and Wand kay Shako* (share what you have with others) were considered essential parts of their culture and daily living. He is a Gold Coast Sikh Association stalwart and has participated in the association's fundraising projects like Desi Night. In addition, he engages actively in religious and meditation services at the Gurdwara Sahib Gold Coast.

Navin is a global banking consultant and prolific writer and editor on a whole range of business and social issues. In 2018, he established the Pasricha Foundation, dedicated to working with organisations focused on bringing better education and health to the poorer segments of Indian society and to battling corruption.

Of the four Pasricha children, the eldest, Arvind Pasricha, graduated from Griffith University on the Gold Coast and then moved to Kuala Lumpur. He is the chief executive officer of a media company with operations in Malaysia and Singapore and he lives with his wife, Ravinder Kaur, and son, Ashvin, in Singapore. Ravinder is a senior executive with the Discovery Channel.

Deepa and Navin's elder daughter, Shivani, gained her PhD in genetics from Melbourne University. She is a postdoctoral research fellow at the Hudson Institute for Medical Research and lives in Melbourne with her husband, Dane Vassilliadis, and their son, Saiyan. Dane is a geneticist and a postdoctoral scientist at the Peter MacCallum Cancer Centre.

Twenty-three-year-old Navdeep Pasricha, the younger son of Navin and Deepa Pasricha, arrived on the Gold Coast in 2009 with his family as a Year Nine student at Somerset College, where he made his mark and was conferred the 'Spirit of Somerset'.

Navdeep was recognised as a community leader at a very early age when he was awarded the 2013 John Franklin Memorial Fellowship, which recognises young community leaders. He also won The India-Australia Business and Community Award in The Young Community Achiever category in 2015. Navdeep's enterprise, drive and never-say-die attitude saw him receive the Channel 7 Young Achiever Award in 2019, in the Change-maker of the Year category.

Whilst studying at Bond University, Navdeep became one of Australia's young entrepreneurs at the age of nineteen when he established a foundation called iYouth and was subsequently voted best entrepreneur by the Bond University Business Accelerator programme. iYouth is dedicated to improving the mental well-being of children, young people, teachers and principals and serves as a vehicle for youth in the Gold Coast to give back to the community. In this journey, Navdeep has already impacted more than twenty thousand people through seminars, counselling and TEDx talks.

Navdeep also owns the Teachflix video platform, which provides remote professional development for teachers and university lecturers and helps them tackle particularly difficult educational areas. He has worked closely with various youth- and education-related bodies in both government and private sectors and sits on the board of a major Gold Coast high school. He has established entrepreneurship programmes in educational establishments in Queensland and New South Wales and has a keen interest in bringing equal educational opportunities to regional Australia.

According to Navdeep, the greatest satisfaction he gets is from the iYouth foundation because it acts as an instrument for Gold Coast youth to work with the local community. Volunteer members of the foundation organise events such as 'Pat and Chat', in which young people visit aged-care facilities with their pets and spend time with the residents. In collaboration with iYouth, several other groups are working to replicate this initiative around Australia. The foundation also has a programme for disabled children to visit gymnasiums, and a 'Surf with the Disabled' programme.

Looking to the future, Navdeep wants to take his successful education and well-being models to other regions, especially countries in South and South-East Asia.

Simran, the youngest of the Pasricha children, completed her secondary education at Somerset College on the Gold Coast and is currently an undergraduate at Griffith University. She is doing a double degree in international affairs and international business. She has been awarded Australian government grants to join delegations to Portugal and Fiji. In Fiji, Simran participated in a project to find solutions to try to stem the country's 'brain-drain'. Simran plans to embark on a career that allows her to make a significant contribution to women's empowerment on a global basis.

At university, Simran is on the leadership team of a student organisation dedicated to improving the career prospects of the student body.

She is a committed activist for the protection of the environment and a highly motivated feminist. In her daily life, she is always working for gender equality and has tasked herself with the challenge of changing the traditional, often stereotypical roles of women within Indian families. She is also deeply involved with the iYouth foundation and has managed several projects aimed at improving the wellbeing of the elderly and the disabled on the Gold Coast.

Simran is also well-known on the Gold Coast as an outstanding jazz and blues singer and performs regularly for fundraising and community events that are close to her heart.

3.2.11 Pushpinder Oberoi

Indian-born Pushpinder Oberoi, or Push as he is often called, became a Gold Coast resident in 1993. He owned and managed a number of Gold Coast Indian restaurants, having done the same in New Zealand prior to moving to Australia, before reducing his workload in 2016. At present, he helps oversee the management of Goa Indian Fusion at Tedder Avenue in the Main Beach area.

In his time here, Push has achieved many Gold Coast Sikh firsts. He was the founder and president of the Gold Coast Indian Cultural Association, which promoted Indian-Australian relationships through business, social and cultural activities. He has been the president of the Global Organisation for People of Indian Origin (GOPIO), Gold Coast Chapter since 2017. The Outstanding Contribution Award was conferred upon him in 2018 for his contributions to the Gold Coast Indian community.

During the Gold Coast Commonwealth Games in 2018, Push was appointed as a liaison officer for the Indian team and was actively involved in promoting sales of tickets for games involving the Indian hockey team.

In 2019, the Diaspora Foundation appointed him as Honorary Ambassador and presented him with an Award of Appreciation for

Contribution in Pioneering Indian Culinary Arts, and an Award of Appreciation, Justice of Peace, Commissioner of Declaration, Indian Community Ambassador.

Push is also the current president of the Non-resident Indian Welfare Society and publicises the achievements and contributions of NRIs (Non-resident Indians) there. He has assisted various Indian High Commissioners to Australia in setting up meetings with community leaders and members, and played a part in running the International Day of Yoga on 29 June 2019, which was organised by the Indian Consulate, Queensland, the Indian High Commission, Canberra, and the Federation of Indian Communities Queensland (FICQ).

In January 2019, Push was invited by the Indian Ministry of External Affairs to attend the Pravasi Bharatiya Divas Convention in Varanasi, India, with the objective of expanding the relationship between India and Australia. This convention aimed to strengthen Australian NRI ties with India and raise the profiles of NRIs who have contributed positively to the countries they migrated to. In addition, he received an invitation from the Indian Ministry of Defence to attend the 2019 Republic Day Parade.

More recently, on 25 January 2020, Pushpinder was honoured with the prestigious Hind Rattan award – an annual award presented to handpicked NRIs, in appreciation of their services to the Indian diaspora. He accepted the Hind Rattan at an annual congress held on the eve of India's Republic Day commemoration, in conjunction with the Indian Pravasi Bharatiya Divas celebrations.

Pushpinder was also appointed Multicultural Ambassador for 2020 by the Mental Health Australia Foundation (MHFA) to assist multicultural and Indigenous communities in mental health and professional development matters.

In addition, Pushpinder had the unique distinction of being awarded a Global Humanitarian Award by the World Humanitarian Drive for his untiring services and support for the benefit of the community during the Covid-19 pandemic. The honour was bestowed on him on 28 June 2020 and he was the only Australian to gain this citation. As president of GOPIO,

Pushpinder kept an eye on the welfare of Indian students affected by Covid-19, counselling those wishing to return to India on the procedures involved. As for those who wanted to stay, he provided advice on food, finance, rent and education matters. Pushpinder kept in close contact with the Office of the Indian High Commissioner, Gold Coast authorities and the Federation of Indian Communities of Queensland (FICQ) throughout the Covid-19 crisis. He also used the premises of Goa Indian Fusion to supply free takeaway vegetarian meal packs to international students affected by Covid-19.

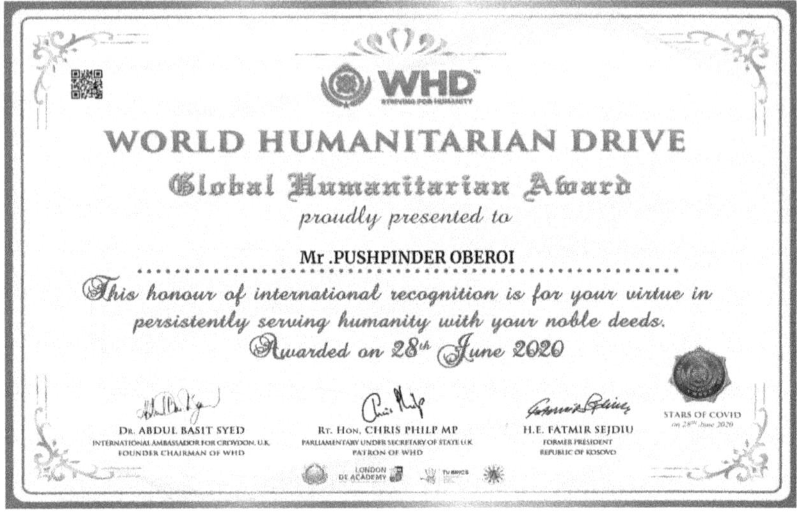

WHD

WORLD HUMANITARIAN DRIVE

Global Humanitarian Award

proudly presented to

Mr .PUSHPINDER OBEROI

This honour of international recognition is for your virtue in persistently serving humanity with your noble deeds.

Awarded on 28th June 2020

DR. ABDUL BASIT SYED

RT. HON. CHRIS PHILP MP

PATRON OF WHD

H.E. FATMIR SEJDIU

STARS OF COVID

Besides his contributions to the wider community, Pushpinder has also involved himself actively in Gold Coast Sikh affairs. He served as a committee member of the Gold Coast Sikh Association between 2012 and 2016 and contributed significantly towards efforts to get Gold Coast City Council's assistance in securing the association's own property.

3.2.12 The Bagga Family

Manmohan Singh Bagga and his wife, Parina Bagga, arrived from India in 1994, together with their daughter, Hashmita Bagga. They came on a student visa as Parina had been accepted into the Master of Business Administration course at Griffith University. Eventually, they decided to call the Gold Coast, and Australia, home.

Manmohan has owned and operated an Indian restaurant, Indian Hut, since 2004.

He is a foundation member and committee member of the Gold Coast Sikh Association, while Parina has been a committee member and treasurer at different times since 2010. Many *langgar seva* events during Gurdwara assemblies since 2005 have been organised by Manmohan's family. They have also participated actively in fundraising initiatives like dinner-and-dance events, and through securing donations for the Gold Coast Sikh Association. An example of their altruism was supplying food and decorations at no cost to the Gold Coast Sikh Association each time the association held the Desi Night fundraising event between 2010 and 2018.

Manmohan and Parina were at the forefront during the Covid-19 pandemic, providing valuable assistance in the form of free vegetarian food to members of the community hardest hit by the resultant lockdown. Their generosity extended to giving volunteers access to their restaurant's kitchen to prepare and cook the food.

In addition to donating time, money and effort to help renovate the Gurdwara Sahib Gold Coast in Nerang, Manmohan additionally donated various types of equipment for the prayer and *langgar* halls. He also provided the Gurdwara with shoe racks and raised seating for congregants who are unable to sit on the floor and has beautified the entrance to the Gurdwara by establishing a flower garden.

Parina was one of the first three graduates of the Guru Granth Sahib Ji Academy's Gurmukhi classes conducted in Robina. For the past four years, she has been teaching Gurmukhi to new students.

Their daughter Hashmita, now Dr Hashmita Bagga, qualified as the first Gold Coast Sikh Dentist in 2011 at Griffith University. She started her own practice from scratch, at a relatively young age of 25 years. She is also a mentor and clinical supervisor for dental students at Griffith University, a position she has held since 2015. Her husband, Navaljyot Josan, owns and operates a pharmacy in Robina. Hashmita often accompanies her younger sister, Jasleen, who was born in 2004, during the singing of *kirtans* at the Gurdwara. Jasleen is in the process of completing her school studies as a Year 12 pupil.

3.2.13 Dr Hargurdip Singh and Family

The Singh family has been living on the Gold Coast since moving here from Newcastle in 1997. Dr Hargurdip and his wife, Janette Singh, chose to settle here for the lifestyle, after living in a few locations along the east coast of Australia. Janette's family roots are mentioned in Chapter 2 (Section 2.6).

Originally from India, Hargurdip has been working as a general practitioner on the Gold Coast for approximately 22 years. His interest in expanding his range of expertise in the field of medicine led him to undertake a course in liposuction (cosmetic surgery) in 1998. Hargurdip acquired a Diploma in Sports Medicine in 2007 and, thereafter, served as a medical professional at sports matches (such as boxing competitions). In 2006, he branched out on his own as a general practitioner on the Gold Coast.

Hargurdip and Australian-born Janette are active members of the community and regularly do *seva* for the *sanggat* (congregation) at the Gurdwara Sahib Gold Coast in Nerang. He was one of the doctors who provided free medical examinations to congregants at the Nerang Gurdwara. He has participated actively in helping to raise funds for the purchase, renovation and running of the Gurdwara along with other members of the committee. Furthermore, he is passionate about singing *shabad* most Sundays at the Gurdwara. Janette is heavily involved in helping organise the kitchen and *langgar seva* each week.

Hargurdip is a sports enthusiast and uses an exercise regime involving social tennis as a means of staying fit.

Pavanjit Singh, Janette and Hargurdip's first child, graduated with First Class Honours in Health Sciences from Bond University in 2015, the first Gold Coast Sikh to achieve this distinction. Her honours research project was based on the potential use of alpha-1 adrenoceptor antagonists as a treatment for bladder cancer. She then moved on to work as a scientific recruitment consultant at Kelly Services before pursuing further study at Monash University. On an extracurricular basis, Pavanjit enjoys bushwalking, singing Bollywood songs and performing Bhangra at events (such as the annual Desi Night for the Gurdwara Sahib).

Pavanjit's younger sister, Priya, is currently completing her third year at Bond University in a double degree of laws and international relations. She completed levels B1 and B2 of the Diploma of French Language Studies as a high school student and has spent time in France on exchange to further her language skills. She was also selected to travel to Japan as part of a team of eleven students to attend the Japan English Model United Nations (JEMUN) Conference in early 2020. Unfortunately, the conference had to be cancelled due to the Covid-19 pandemic.

3.2.14 The Patheja Family

Dr Sukhbir Singh Patheja and his wife, Leena Kaur Patheja, together with their two young children, Rajan Singh Patheja and Simran Kaur Patheja, moved to Australia from the United Kingdom in 1995 and worked in Perth, Brisbane and Central Queensland before making the Gold Coast their home in 1997. Sukhbir settled into general practice in the Parkwood-Arundel area, where he still works. Leena commenced work as an optometrist, thereby becoming the first Sikh optometrist to operate on the Gold Coast. Their youngest child, Amar Singh Patheja, was born in 2001.

Their first child, Rajan, went to school at Somerset College, where he excelled – he has a remarkable number of Gold Coast Sikh community firsts to his name. In addition to representing the school in numerous sporting and academic undertakings, he was the first Sikh school captain at Somerset College. He graduated from school with an Overall Position (OP) score of 1, another Gold Coast Sikh first. An OP1 is the highest score for a Queensland Year 12 graduate, a score achieved by only about 2% of Queensland school-leavers. Rajan went on to complete a degree in medicine at the University of New South Wales, graduating with First Class Honours and adding another Gold Coast Sikh first to his name. He is currently completing his training as an ophthalmologist and will be the first Gold Coast Sikh ophthalmologist, upon graduation. Rajan is married to Ananya Patheja and hopes to establish himself on the Gold Coast.

Sukhbir and Leena's daughter, Simran, also went to school at Somerset College, where she was awarded a half scholarship. Like her older sibling, she secured an OP1 in her Year 12 examinations, the first Gold Coast Sikh girl to achieve this feat. She was awarded a full scholarship to study dentistry at the University of Queensland and is currently a practising dentist in Brisbane. Simran plans to return to the Gold Coast, with the aim of practising in the Gold Coast Public Dental Services.

Amar, the youngest of the family, also completed schooling at Somerset College and went on to study for a double degree in commerce and information technology at Griffith University. He is an active sportsman and occasionally plays basketball for a local representative team.

The Patheja family are part of the Lions Club initiative to help the needy in Eldoret, Kenya. They make frequent visits to that part of the world to donate wheelchairs to those who need them. Dr Rajan hopes, eventually, to contribute surgical expertise to help the poor with free cataract surgery through the Lions Club. The family's sense of service has also seen them contribute generously towards the establishment of the two existing Gurdwaras on the Gold Coast.

3.2.15 Dr Raja Sawhney

London-born Dr Raja Sawhney MBBS FRACS (PLAST) received his medical degree from Guy's and St Thomas' Hospitals at the relatively young age of twenty-two. One of his early achievements was being appointed Demonstrator of Surgical Anatomy at the eminent Anatomy School of Guy's Hospital.

He left the UK for Australia in 1998 on a working holiday and after working in various Queensland hospitals, settled down on the Gold Coast.

Raja started out as an orthopaedic surgeon and he also did general, cardiac and transplant surgery before eventually becoming a plastic, reconstructive and cosmetic surgeon, the first Gold Coast Sikh to acquire this status. He specialises in rectifying physical imperfections caused by cancer or trauma and conducts breast surgery, facelift, rhinoplasty, nerve reconstruction and hand surgery. To Raja, reconstructive and cosmetic surgeries are not just scientific and academic but also artistic. He played a central role in the establishment of a broad-based unit to cater for breast, head, neck and lower-limb reconstruction.

Raja is a well-qualified plastic surgeon of repute and is a member of the Australasian Society of Aesthetic Plastic Surgeons (ASAPS) and is professionally associated with the Royal Australasian Colleges of Surgery (RACS) and the Australian Board of Plastic and Reconstructive Surgery. He is the Director of Plastic and Reconstructive Surgery at the Gold Coast University Hospital and Robina Hospital. He is also the Director of Sculpted Clinic. Most of his surgical work is conducted at the Gold Coast Private Hospital and he has admitting rights at Pindara Hospital, John Flynn Hospital and Brisbane Private Hospital.

3.2.16 The Saini Family

Jaspreet Saini left India for Australia and stepped foot on the Gold Coast in January 1999. He has a degree in electrical engineering (electronics) from Dharwad University, Karnatka, India, and a postgraduate degree (Master of Information Technology) from Bond University, Gold Coast.

Jaspreet has been an active participant in community activities on the Gold Coast, having served two separate terms on the committee of the Gold Coast Sikh Association. He was the association's treasurer in his first term. He played a role in the setting up of the Nerang Gurdwara Sahib Gold Coast and has taken on the responsibility of developing the association's website.

Jaspreet is a keep-fit enthusiast and counts badminton and cricket as his main sporting pursuits.

Jaspreet's wife, Anudeep Kaur Sidhu, hails from Abohar, Punjab,

India. She has been in Australia since 2002 and has two masters degrees: a Master of Business Administration from the Punjab Technical University, and a Master of Accounting from the University of Western Sydney. She moved to the Gold Coast in 2013 after her marriage to Jaspreet and works as an accountant and financial analyst. Jaspreet and Amandeep have a two-year-old son, Zoraver Saini.

3.2.17 The SS Gill Family

Sanjiv Singh Gill, his wife, Surinder, and their baby daughter, Grishwin, left Singapore for the Gold Coast in 2003, although Surinder had visited a year earlier. It is quite probable that they are the first Singaporean family of the Sikh faith to make the Gold Coast their home.

According to Sanjiv, Surinder has always been the focal point of the family through her support of him and their children (their second child, Jayvir Singh Gill, was born on the Gold Coast). A trained nurse, she worked in the intensive care unit of Hospital Fatimah, Ipoh, Malaysia, before having her contract bought out by Gleneagles Hospital, Singapore, after her marriage to Sanjiv. She then worked in the intensive care unit of Gleneagles for two years before the family left for Australia. She secured a Bachelor of Nursing degree from Griffith University on the Gold Coast in 2004, to complement her Malaysian nursing qualification, and joined the intensive care unit at the Allamanda Private Hospital in the same year. Surinder moved to the Robina Hospital's intensive care unit in 2015, where she works at present.

In addition to his appreciation of his wife's support, Sanjiv is indebted to his late father, Pritam Singh Gill, for his assistance in helping him and his family settle down in Pacific Pines on the Gold Coast.

Sanjiv has worked in the hotel industry since he was a teenager. He secured his first job at Apollo Hotel on Havelock Road in Singapore when he was seventeen and continued along the same lines when he came to the Gold Coast at the age of thirty-two. His employers here have been The Hyatt, Jupiter's Casino and Royal Pines.

Sanjiv has been actively involved with the Gold Coast Sikh community, regularly volunteering his assistance during Gurdwara assemblies by way of helping set up the prayer and *langgar* halls, assisting in the communal kitchen and cleaning and tidying up at the end of the day, in addition to participating in religious services during assemblies.

Grishwin completed her schooling at Pacific Pines School and Queensland Academy Gold Coast. She is currently in her first year of dental studies at Griffith University and hopes to establish herself as a successful dentist on the Gold Coast.

Grishwin's brother, Jayvir, is in Year 9 at Pacific Pines Gold Coast. He is an avid soccer player and has represented the Gold Coast United under-14s team – the first Gold Coast Sikh child to do so.

Jayvir was also the first Sikh infant to be baptised according to Sikh rites (*Amrit Sanchar)* on the Gold Coast. The ceremony was conducted in 2006 when the Gold Coast Sikh community used to meet for meditation at the Robina Community Centre.

3.2.18 The Kaurah Family

Indian-born Kuldip Singh Kaurah arrived on the Gold Coast in 2003, together with his wife, Malaysian-born Jessy Kaurah, and sons, Daman and Jasdip. He started his own carpet-cleaning business, which he runs to this day, serving clients all over the Gold Coast and Brisbane.

Kuldip is a foundation member of the Gold Coast Sikh Association and has also been a committee member of the association since its inception in 2010. He was also the association's president from 2012 to 2013. The association owes Kuldip a debt of gratitude for his unfailing service from 2005 to 2018 in helping to transport equipment and configure the set-up of the assembly hall at the Robina Community Centre.

Kuldip has involved himself actively in fundraising projects like Desi Night and has regularly performed community services linked to Gold Coast Sikhs. His *seva* during Gurdwara assemblies goes a long way towards ensuring that everything progresses smoothly. He played an important role in the renovation and maintenance of the Nerang Gurdwara Sahib Gold Coast.

Jessy Kaurah has also been on the committee as treasurer. She contributed enormously towards the success of numerous Gold Coast Sikh Association's Desi Night events, particularly by organising the selling of tickets, ensuring that ticket sales and monies collected matched, following up on IOUs (monies owed to the Gold Coast Sikh Association), and working on income-expense spreadsheets.

Jessy has been in the banking industry for the past twenty years and is also an appointed Commissioner of Declaration for the Queensland Government. Her favourite pastime is baking decorative cakes for all occasions.

Every member of the Kaurah family has contributed broadly to the religious and social activities of the association's Gurdwara. Their contributions include setting up for assemblies and tidying up at the end of each assembly, looking after and cleaning carpet-sheets, storing Gurdwara implements such as speakers and electrical items, providing *langgar seva* and fundraising. Daman and Jasdip have also been regular *kirtan* singers during Gurdwara assemblies. In addition, Kuldip and Jessy have played important roles in the renovation process since the purchase of the association's Gurdwara building in Nerang.

Daman is currently in his final year as a student of actuarial science at Bond University. He is a keen basketball player, having represented his school, Varsity College, and Gold Coast Basketball Club for a few years.

Jasdip completed Year 12 at Varsity College, securing an Overall Position (OP) of 2, the second-highest Queensland Year 12 grade. He is also an avid basketball player and, like his older brother Daman, has played for his school and the Gold Coast Basketball Club. Jasdip is enrolled in a Bachelor of Medical Imaging course at the Queensland University of Technology, Brisbane. He has also accepted an offer from Bond University, Gold Coast, to read medicine at the Faculty of Health Sciences and Medicine from September 2020.

3.2.19 The Rajpal Family

Japjit Singh Rajpal, also known as Jaimie, arrived on the Gold Coast in 2003 from India on a student visa to study a Master of Information

Technology at Griffith University, having already secured a Bachelor of Commerce in India. Possessing a keen interest in information technology, he attended courses in web-designing and computer hardware in India in preparation for his postgraduate course in Australia.

While on the Gold Coast, he supported himself as a delivery driver for a Maries Pizza franchise from 2003. His dedication and hard work resulted in his promotion to manager within six months of joining the company. Over time, he developed a passion for making pizzas, with the aim of owning his own pizza outlet down the track. His dream came to fruition when, on 17 January 2011, he bought his first pizza shop as a franchise from Maries Pizza in Runaway Bay. At its peak, his franchise had eight workers in total. Japjit did all his training at the head office of Maries Pizza. He ran the Runaway Bay outlet until May 2016, when he decided to pursue other interests, including starting a point of sale (POS) business connected to Xpert Tech Solutions to help him stay up to date with his information technology background. He still runs the business, which involves buying and selling new and used POS systems.

In November 2018, Japjit decided to re-enter the pizza business and opened his own pizza shop called Best Bite Pizza in Upper Coomera. Within three months of opening, his shop won tenth position in a pizza shop survey of the top ten Gold Coast pizza outlets, as conducted by the Gold Coast Bulletin in 2019. He surpassed this achievement in 2020 when Best Bite Pizza was voted the number one pizza shop – a first for the Gold Coast Sikh community.

Japjit is married to Mandeep Kaur, who is a registered nurse. They have two children, an eight-year-old son, Guransh Rajpal and a three-year-old daughter, Gurmehar Rajpal.

When he is not at work or indulging in his favourite pastimes involving drone-racing, cars and motorbikes, Japjit participates in community work when required. He hopes to pass on his work ethic to his children, to help them create avenues for themselves and achieve success in their adult lives as Sikh Australians.

3.2.20 The Bains Family

Bhajan Singh Bains, who is of Malaysian background, has been another major contributor to the development of the Gold Coast Sikh community. Bhajan and his wife, Manjit Kaur, and their two young children, Preety Kaur Bains and Gobind Singh Bains, arrived in 2004.

Bhajan started a carpet cleaning business shortly after setting foot on the Gold Coast – the first Sikh to do so. In another first for the community, he qualified as a turbaned registered male Sikh nurse in 2009. Previously, he had served as an enrolled nurse (in Melbourne, starting 1999). His success in the nursing field inspired at least two other Sikhs (Amrit Kaur Bhorla and Balpreet Kaur Hayer) to become registered nurses.

On 11 June 2005, Bhajan, a deeply committed Sikh, became the first Gold Coast *Granthi* to conduct prayers at the first-ever Sikh assembly to be held at a place that was not a private home – the Robina Community Centre. This gathering led to many more, resulting in the formation of the Gold Coast Sikh Association and culminating in the establishment of an official Gurdwara in Nerang.

In 2006, Bhajan presided over the very first *Amrit Sanchar* ceremony on the Gold Coast for newborn Jayvir Singh, the son of Sanjiv Singh Gill and Surinder Kaur.

In 2017, he accepted the position of Director of the Gold Coast Sikh Council and played an important role in the establishment of the first Gurdwara to be constructed from the ground up. He was one of the *Punj Pyaaray* involved in the Gold Coast's first ground-breaking ceremony for that Gurdwara.

Like her husband, Manjit moved from Malaysia to Australia. One of ten siblings, she has strong religious leanings and a deep sense of civic-mindedness. She is not only a devoted wife and mother with culinary skills to keep the family happy, but also a health provider, practising as an enrolled nurse for the last 30 years. Manjit is the oldest sister in her family while Jessy Kaur Kaurah (mentioned in 3.2.19) is the youngest.

Since Bhajan and Manjit's son, Gobind Singh Bains, was a teenager, he has contributed considerably to the Gold Coast Sikh community's gatherings by singing *kirtan*. He went on to complete his tertiary studies in business at Bond University before securing a job in Brisbane. Gobind is also one of the first three graduates of the Guru Granth Sahib Ji Academy's course in Gurmukhi on the Gold Coast. He recently became the first turbaned Sikh to serve as a paramedic on the Gold Coast. He and his wife, Jessie Kaur Bains, have a young daughter named Mahee Kaur Bains.

Bhajan and Manjit's daughter, Preety Kaur Bains, was the first Gold Coast Sikh to secure a bursary from Bond University to pursue studies in law. She served as committee member of the Gold Coast Sikh Association in 2014 and 2015 and played a major part in the planning and running of fundraising events, particularly Desi Night, an annual dinner and dance function. She currently works as a lawyer on the Gold Coast. Preety has also been part of the Young Sikh Professional Network (YSPN), an initiative of Sikh Youth Australia. The YSPN and Sikh Youth Australia put together a report in 2016 that stated that Sikh Australians contribute $8.1 billion to the Gross Domestic Product (Arora & Singh, 2019). The

YSPN is a not-for-profit organisation that seeks to raise the profile of young Sikh professionals and enhance their positive impact on society. Preety has, among other undertakings, helped organise talks on behalf of YSPN.

3.2.21 The Dillon Family

Jagmohanbir Singh Dillon, (often shortened to Jagmohan or Mony), arrived on the Gold Coast in 2005. His wife, Kelwant Kaur, and their three children, Charndpreet Kaur Dillon, Baldev Raj Singh Dillon and Manpreet Kaur Dillon, came soon after. Jagmohanbir and Kelwant were both originally from Malaysia.

Jagmohanbir is a foundation member and committee member of the Gold Coast Sikh Association. He held the position of president of the Gold Coast Sikh Association from 2017 to 2018.

He was the first tabla player during the early days when Sikh prayer ceremonies were held informally at the Robina Community Centre. It is a service Jagmohanbir still provides at the Gurdwara Sahib Gold Coast in Nerang.

Jagmohanbir's participation in fundraising activities for the association – including securing approval from the Gold Coast City Council and sourcing engineers for town-planning requirements – has helped accelerate the establishment of the Gurdwara in Nerang.

His academic qualifications include a Master of Business Administration from the University of Canberra and a PhD in Cardiovascular Pharmacology from the University of Melbourne. He partnered in the establishment and management of a medical-devices company that was listed on the Stock Exchange, retiring after ten years to move to the Gold Coast. While in Canberra, Jagmohanbir was a member of the Canberra Sikh Association and actively participated in securing land from the Australian Capital Territory (ACT) Government for the establishment of a Gurdwara.

Shortly after arriving on the Gold Coast, Jagmohanbir ventured into the world of property development. After a few years, he moved away from the property business and established himself as a shade-sails and awnings entrepreneur, the first Gold Coast Sikh in this line of business. His company currently has a staff of seven.

Kelwant Kaur trained as a dentist at Manipal University in India. Upon her return to Australia, she joined the Australian Government Therapeutic Goods Administration, as a medical and dental devices regulator. At present, she is working as a carer with an aged care provider. Kelwant is also one of the first three graduates of the Guru Granth Sahib Ji Academy's Gurmukhi course held in Robina and now teaches Gurmukhi to children and adults.

Charndpreet, their eldest child, qualified as an optometrist from Deakin University in Geelong, Victoria. She currently works as a consulting optometrist.

Their son, Baldev Raj, has a degree in commerce/law from Griffith University on the Gold Coast. He is a graduate intern with a government agency at present.

Their youngest child, Manpreet, also graduated from Griffith University, with a Bachelor of Sports Science. She is now furthering her training in nutrition and dietetics.

3.2.22 Dr Harpreet Singh

Dr Harpreet Singh, or Harry as he is often called, arrived on the Gold Coast in March 2006 and was the first Sikh paediatrician and paediatric neurologist here. He secured his BSc MBBS from Shimla Himachal Pradesh and worked in Shimla as a medical officer. Following that, he moved to the United Kingdom and trained in paediatrics for five years, after which he was given the title Member of the Royal College of Paediatrics and Child Health (MRCPCH) associated with the Royal College of Physicians, United Kingdom. Harry then pursued further paediatric training in Wellington, New Zealand, for another five years and, upon completion, moved to Australia for higher sub-speciality training involving paediatric neurology. After receiving this qualification, he moved to the Gold Coast, eventually establishing and managing a paediatric neurology service at the Gold Coast University Hospital.

At present, Harry works as a paediatric neurologist at the Gold Coast University Hospital. He has also set up a private paediatric and brain centre on the Gold Coast and has been instrumental in bringing various specialists to work in this centre. Besides his MRCPCH, he is also a Fellow of the Royal Australasian College of Physicians (FRACP).

In addition to his medical practice, he is an associate professor and paediatric lead at Bond University. Harry visits India frequently to participate in charity work and to provide support to children in Shimla, his place of origin and a well-known holiday destination in the Himalayas.

Harry is a keen sports enthusiast, particularly in table tennis; he won the All-India Medical College table tennis championship for seven consecutive years during his student days. In addition, he was a state champion and represented his state in national-level competitions. Harry has maintained his involvement with table tennis by participating in high-level competitions here in Australia.

Lindsay Singh, Harry's wife, used to work as a nurse but now holds the position of manager at Harry's private practice. She is a keen artist and dabbles in interior decoration as a hobby.

Their daughter, Grace Singh, is currently completing her medical studies at Bond University and expects to graduate at the end of 2020. Her ambition is to specialise in the care and wellness of children.

Harry's father, Joginder Singh Meet, is a renowned poet in India and has recited his poetry in the presence of various national leaders since his early years. Among these leaders was India's first Prime Minister, Jawahar Lal Nehru. Meet (Joginder's nom de plume), who is 91 years old, has written several thousand poems, many of which deal with the depth and scope of elements of Sikh culture. A deeply religious person, he references God and spirituality in his poems regularly. His poetry also deals with political, social and family matters and has a wide range of tones, including serious, philosophical, satirical, and comical. Originally from Shimla, Meet now resides with Harry on the Gold Coast and often recites his religious poetry at Gurdwaras on the Gold Coast and in Brisbane.

Harry's brother, Jaswinder Singh, retired recently from his position as Professor of English in Himachal Pradesh University Colleges. He was a prominent table tennis player in his younger days, having emulated his brother in winning a state championship in India. Jaswinder has three children: two daughters, Dr Jasleen Katial and Dr Simran Katial who are dentists in India, and a son, Angad Katial, who is studying architecture at Griffith University on the Gold Coast while representing the Gold Coast Dolphins Cricket Club. Angad hopes to become a property developer. Dr Simran Katial, Jaswinder's younger daughter, is expected to move to the Gold Coast soon.

3.2.23 The Bhorla Family

Ranbir Singh Bhorla and his family have been living in Mudgeeraba since 2007. He first came to Australia from India in May 1987 after completing his pre-engineering degree from DAV College in Jalandhar. He joined his brother, Kulbir Singh Bhorla, who had migrated a year earlier. Their father, Kundan Singh, had held important positions before he passed away, prior to Ranbir's departure for Australia. He had served as *Sarpanch* (a person elected by the village authorities as their decision-maker and the main link between the villagers and the government) of his village for 25 years. In addition, he was on the Municipal Council of Nawanshahr for five years. Nawanshahr is famous for its association with India's freedom fighter Bhagat Singh, who fought against the British Raj.

Ranbir and Kulbir initially lived with their grandfather, Karam Singh Bhorla, in Natural Bridge, a Gold Coast locality that is part of Springbrook National Park. Their grandfather, who had arrived in Australia in 1936, owned a dairy farm there and Ranbir and Kulbir helped him and their uncles, Bhajan Singh Bhorla and Darshan Singh Bhorla, with chores at the farm.

Ranbir and Kulbir moved to Murwillumbah three months later, having purchased a banana farm there. Shortly after his grandfather passed away in April 1990, Ranbir returned to India. There, he met and married his wife, Amrit Bhorla, who arrived in Australia in 1992. The married couple and their family moved from Murwillumbah to Terranora in 1995 and later, in 2007, relocated to Mudgeeraba. Amrit, who has a Master of Nursing degree, is a registered nurse. She worked at the Robina Hospital for six years and at the Griffith University Hospital for a few months in 2015.

Ranbir's sibling Kulbir currently lives in Brisbane, his uncle Bhajan lives in Coomera, a Gold Coast suburb, while his uncle Darshan owns a dairy farm in Kyogle, New South Wales. His mother, Madam Surinder Kaur, lives with him and his family. She makes regular trips to India to keep in touch with the wider family there. Ranbir has two sisters who both live in Canada and he also has relatives in North Queensland, Sydney and Melbourne.

Ranbir and Amrit have two sons. Their older son, Karanveer Bhorla, is in his final year of a course in plumbing at a Technical and Further Education (TAFE) training provider in Benowa, a Gold Coast suburb. He also works with a company called Ocean Plumbing. Jasrun Bhorla, their younger son, is studying to be a pharmacist and is currently in his second year at Griffith University.

Ranbir has been running a taxi business on the Gold Coast since 2001. He is well-respected and has quite a high profile within the Sikh communities of Murwillumbah, Woolgoolga, the Gold Coast and Brisbane because of his dedicated involvement in community service and Gurdwara fundraising initiatives. His presence at numerous social and religious functions makes him a very familiar figure in Sikh community circles, both young and senior. He is generous with his time when it comes to doing *seva* for the benefit of Sikhs. For example, despite being a Gold Coast resident, Ranbir finds the time to be an active part of the Murwillumbah Sikh community and serves on the Murwillumbah Gurdwara Sahib Ji as secretary, driving more than 40 kilometres to get there each time his services are required.

A firm believer in service for the welfare of the disadvantaged, Ranbir willingly extended a helping hand as soon as the 2020 Covid-19 pandemic approached a critical stage. Not only did he participate fully in the Murwillumbah Sikh Temple's project of supplying free takeaway vegetarian food every day to those afflicted by the lockdown, he personally delivered meals and ingredients (like flour and rice) to those in the surrounding area who were unable to travel to the Sikh Temple. In one instance, Ranbir travelled as far as Brunswick Heads, about 33 kilometres away from Murwillumbah, to deliver food to international students.

His humanitarian traits were also in evidence on the Gold Coast, where he helped deliver vegetarian meals to frontline medical staff at the Gold Coast University Hospital and Robina Hospital, as well as families quarantined at Voco Hotel and QT Hotel. He was ably supported by Surjit Singh Dhillon of Tandoori Place in his tireless efforts in Murwillumbah and the Gold Coast – Surjit cooked the meals for the recipients. Ranbir's exceptional altruism extended to his reaching into his own pocket to help purchase groceries during the crisis. To date, he and Surjit are still involved in the Covid-19-associated charitable work.

3.2.24 The Sahota Family

One of the Gold Coast Sikh Association's occasional *kirtan* singers, Raminder Singh Sahota, set up home on the Gold Coast in 2007. A Bachelor of Engineering (Electronics) graduate of Mysore University in India and holder of a Master of Engineering degree, by research, from the University of South Australia, he works as a telecoms engineer on the Gold Coast. He has also held the position of engineering manager in Hutchison, Ericsson, Vodafone, and Pivotel for their cellular network rollouts.

Raminder often lends his expertise in video and audio recordings for special events, such as Desi Night, organised by the Gold Coast Sikh Association.

His wife, Tamara, has worked as a sales representative and vitamin consultant. Raminder and Tamara have three children: Simrati, who is a pharmacist and currently studying for a Master of Medical Research at Griffith University, and Arjan and Rajeet, both in Benowa High School in Years 11 and 10 respectively.

3.2.25 Dr Maninder Singh and Family

Dr Maninder Singh and his wife, Dr Prabhjot Kaur Singh, left India and made the Gold Coast their home in 2008.

Maninder was the first Sikh to work as a respiratory specialist at the Gold Coast University Hospital, where he is the assistant director of respiratory and sleep medicine. After completing his specialist training in Brisbane, he and his family moved to the Gold Coast in March 2008. Through knowledge gained from workshops in Singapore, Malaysia and Europe, he initiated the interventional pulmonary services at the Gold Coast University Hospital. Maninder also took his medical expertise to an Aboriginal outreach clinic in Cherbourg, Queensland, where he provided voluntary specialist respiratory services between 2012 and 2018. He is an associate professor of medicine at Griffith and Bond Universities.

Maninder is also the treasurer of Friends of Ludhiana (FOL), Queensland branch. In this capacity, he organises fundraising events annually for his alma mater, the Christian Medical College (CMC), Ludhiana. CMC is a missionary college that was established in 1881 by Edith Brown and until 1953 was reserved for women. The aim of the college has always been to help the poor, especially women, of India. The funds Maninder helps raise go towards aiding poor patients and buying medical equipment, including ambulances. The college recently began a motorcycle-ambulance service. This service is particularly useful because of easy manoeuvrability through traffic congestions.

Maninder is actively involved with the Gold Coast Sikh community – he is a foundation and committee member of the Gold Coast Sikh Association and has contributed his time and finances towards the establishment of the Gurdwara Sahib Gold Coast in Nerang. Maninder is deeply committed to ensuring that the Nerang Gurdwara succeeds as an inspiring place of worship for Sikhs and is always at the forefront of activities that benefit the community. He participated in a charitable event at the Nerang Gurdwara in which members of the *sanggat* were given free medical examinations. Furthermore, he served as a frontline doctor with great dedication during the height of the Covid-19 pandemic.

Dr Prabhjot Kaur Singh, Maninder's wife, possesses a Doctorate in Health Services Management. She is a keen academic with a string of qualifications. Dr Prabhjot started with a Bachelor of Science in Nursing, a degree in which she scored distinctions in all her subjects, leading her to win the University Gold Medal and the Presidential Medal in India. She went on to complete postgraduate studies in health administration and research in the United Kingdom, followed by a Doctorate of Health Service Management in Australia. Her other achievements include an Honours Degree in Psychology following a Graduate Diploma in Psychology, and recently, a Graduate Diploma in Teaching (Secondary), specialising in diverse learners (special education) and science.

Prabhjot's work-history spans the fields of health, aged-care, disability and education. She is passionate about public policy and how it interfaces with the day-to-day life of people, and she is proud to have had a long career in public service. She firmly believes in humanitarian work and in serving the broader community and those in need. Both her aid-oriented nature and keen interest in mental health, domestic violence and other social issues have led to her volunteering at Lifeline as a crisis supporter. She is also an ardent advocate of equal opportunities for women.

Prabhjot helped organise a free medical camp at the Gurdwara Sahib Gold Coast, Nerang and, in February 2020, she and Maninder initiated a successful garage sale and raffle at the Nerang Gurdwara Sahib Gold Coast to help raise funds for victims of Australian bushfires that had raged through the country in the previous months. She also helps her husband in fundraising activities for CMC Ludhiana

Annika Singh, the daughter of Maninder and Prabhjot, was born in Australia in 2009. She became the youngest-ever performer to participate in the Gold Coast Sikh Association's series of Desi Nights when she took part in the event in 2014 at the age of five. She is a keen musician, with an interest in the harmonium, flute and piano. She is also a singer and was selected by her school (A. B. Patterson) to undergo voice-training and singing organised by the State Honours Ensemble Programme (SHEP). In 2019, she won first prize in a singing competition organized by her school. Annika is currently the junior captain of her school softball team (2020).

3.2.26 The Chandi Family

Balvinder Singh Chandi, or Balli for short, arrived with his family in January 2008 from Patiala in the Punjab. He and his wife, Gurinderpal Kaur, have a young son, Nischay Singh.

Balvinder is in the car-maintenance industry and owns an automotive workshop, which he has been running since 2016. His workshop, incidentally, is next door to the Nerang Gurdwara Sahib Gold Coast.

Through donations and participation in renovations, Balvinder has been a major contributor to the Gurdwara. He helped with the paintwork, interior design, security camera installation and making the surrounding area, including car-parking, suitable for use.

Balvinder became a committee member of the Gold Coast Sikh

Association in 2018 and helped raise the profile of the Gurdwara by promoting it online and on Facebook, particularly by posting videos of hymn-singing and on-going renovations. He is, in effect, in charge of public relations for the association.

Balvinder contributes towards *langgar* by providing food, helping to prepare and serve *langgar* and serving guests tea and snacks. Given the proximity of his place of work to the Gurdwara, he has taken on the responsibility of unlocking and locking up the building and decorating it for special religious events and social festivities.

His nephew, Maninder Singh, assists him when required. He lent a hand at the preliminary stage of the renovation of the Gurdwara, particularly through paintwork and carpet-laying. Occasionally, he assists in the preparation of *langgar* for assemblies and helps tidy up after assemblies.

3.2.27 Navaljyot Singh Josan

Navaljyot, or Nav, was a high-achieving schoolboy in India, topping Year 10 in science and representing his school in debating. After completing his schooling, he enrolled at the Jamia Hamdard University in Delhi, where he studied pharmacy. He represented his university in cricket, badminton and debating.

After graduating with a Bachelor of Pharmacy degree, Nav left India for the Gold Coast in 2009 and began a Master of Pharmacy at Griffith University. He completed his postgraduate studies successfully in 2012 and ended up making the Gold Coast his home. He married Dr Hashmita Bagga in 2014. In 2016, Nav became the co-owner of a pharmacy, Robina Parkway Chempro – the first turbaned Sikh to do so.

Nav is a committed practitioner of humanitarian Sikh values, whether in the Gurdwara, at home or at work. To this end, his pharmacy participates in a programme that assists mental health patients who have been discharged from hospital. The pharmacy provides these patients with a free Webster-pack service that packs tablets and capsules in clearly labelled blister packs, to ensure patients take the prescribed dosages correctly. Due to his efforts to ensure his store is run efficiently, it was awarded The Best Growth Store of the Year in 2018.

In contribution to the Sikh community, Nav has helped raise awareness among local Sikhs about Gurdwara services and played an important role in raising funds for the purchase, renovation and upkeep of the Gurdwara Sahib Gold Coast in Nerang.

Nav has also served as secretary of the Gold Coast Sikh Association and participated in stage performances at fundraising events like Desi Night. In addition, his service-oriented approach means he often helps organise proceedings during Sunday services at the Gurdwara Sahib Gold Coast.

3.2.28 Maninderjit Singh Kala

Maninderjit Singh Kala, popularly referred to as Mannu Kala, was born in 1984 in Baramulla, Jammu and Kashmir, India. He has a Bachelor of Physiotherapy degree from Santosh Medical University near Delhi, India. He was a student leader at university and fought for student reforms relating to ragging in colleges and universities in North India.

Mannu arrived on the Gold Coast in 2009 to pursue postgraduate studies. After successfully securing two masters degrees from Griffith University, Gold Coast, he joined the Department of Health as a project officer.

With his eyes firmly set on a future in business, Mannu moved on from his position as a government employee to help start Medlab Pathology Queensland in 2016. From humble beginnings, with limited collection centres and only a few employees, Medlab Pathology Queensland grew to be one the largest privately owned pathology companies in Queensland, with around ninety centres and almost three hundred employees.

In 2019, Mannu diversified his expertise and became director and co-owner of Australia's fastest growing skincare and cosmetic company, SKINO2. Since his involvement, the company has successfully established itself in prestigious pharmacies in Australia and is also working on expanding its presence in the Middle East and India.

Mannu's other achievements include being invited to accompany Australia's Trade, Investment and Tourism Minister, Simon Birmingham, on an official business mission to India as part of the AIB-X programme (Australia Indian Business Exchange), and to represent the Gold Coast as an official ambassador of 'Destination Gold Coast' to promote the Gold Coast in India.

As a community-leader, Mannu involves himself in welfare projects designed to assist those in need. For example, he was the moving force behind the formation of Our Health Vikas, a voluntary charitable health initiative that promotes preventative health medicine and the well-being of the Gold Coast community.

Mannu has also served the Sikh community as a committee member of the Gold Coast Sikh Association. He played an important role in fundraising through events like Desi Night and participation in entertainment programmes. Mannu was also key to the establishment of the Gold Coast Guru Maneyo Granth Gurdwara in Helensvale. As a further measure of his energetic engagement with societal undertakings, he is a founding member of The Global Organisation of People of Indian Origin (GOPIO), Gold Coast chapter.

As a result of Mannu's entrepreneurial achievements, he was presented with a young entrepreneur award from GOPIO Oceania. He was also one of the finalists for a community leader award at The Indian Australian Business and Community Awards (IABCA), 2016.

Most of Mannu's ventures and achievements, as listed previously, represent Gold Coast Sikh firsts.

Mannu is a sports enthusiast, having played state-level basketball and hockey in India. In addition, he has represented Mudgeeraba Cricket Club on the Gold Coast in grade cricket. He is married to Dr Kuljit Singh (whose achievements are discussed in Chapter 3.2.3) and they have two daughters, Anishka, who is seven years old, and Jiya, who is four. The children achieved a Gold Coast and Australian first when they appeared on a YouTube Kids4Kids musical video about coronavirus awareness.

3.2.29 The Mutti Family

Dr Randhir Singh Mutti moved to the Gold Coast from Darwin in 2012 with his wife, Inderjit Kaur, after retiring as a senior medical officer (psychiatry) at the Northern Territory Mental Health Services.

While living and working in Darwin between 1991 and 2012 – after he and Inderjit moved there from India – he dedicated himself not only to his professional responsibilities but also to his devotion to Sikhism. Randhir's adherence to his faith saw him acquire a copy of the Guru Granth Sahib Ji in 1991, thereby providing a place of worship in his house for local Sikhs for more than fifteen years. He served as president and priest of the Sikh Association of Northern Territory and played a major role in securing land from the Northern Territory government on which to build a Gurdwara.

Randhir was a close associate of Tajinder pal Singh, Australian of the Year series (Northern Territory Local Hero) 2017 award-winner, often advising him on relevant matters. In addition, he had close ties with the chief minister of the Northern Territory, partly through the achievements of his daughter, Reetu Kamal Mutti, who was one of the top twenty students in the Northern Territory.

Since his relocation to the Gold Coast, he has participated actively in the local Sikh community's social and religious activities and is currently serving a second term as president of the Gold Coast Sikh Association. In the two years that he has been at the helm, the association has gone from strength to strength. A Gurdwara (Gurdwara Sahib Gold Coast) has been established and weekly assemblies are being held, as compared to the fortnightly or monthly assemblies before the Gurdwara property was purchased. Randhir personally participated in renovating the building and bringing it up to its present pristine state. During the Covid-19 pandemic, he led by example as president of the Gold Coast Sikh Association, working tirelessly to ensure that food reached frontline hospital staff and those affected by the lockdown.

Inderjit, Randhir's wife, who has a Master of Botany (Honours) and a Bachelor of Education, was a lecturer in education before moving to

Australia with Randhir. She worked for the Northern Territory Education Department as a Year 11 and 12 teacher. Inderjit received mathematics and teacher-training qualifications from Charles Darwin University, following which she was appointed to teach Year 10, 11 and 12 children in Indigenous communities via distance-learning. She, too, retired in 2012 and moved to the Gold Coast with Randhir.

Inderjit and Randhir's daughter, Reetu Kamal Mutti, was a high achiever at Dripstone High School in Darwin. She scored high grades in her exams, including achieving a high distinction in a Year 12 subject while she was still in Year 11. Her position as one of the top twenty Year 12 students resulted in her being awarded two scholarships, one from Charles Darwin University and the other from the Northern Territory Education Department. Reetu was honoured for her success by being invited, together with her parents, to a formal ceremony at Parliament House, Northern Territory. She went on to complete a degree in computer programming at Charles Darwin University.

After working in Darwin for two years, Reetu moved to Sydney to join her brother, Upinderdeep, who was studying a Master of Geological Information Systems degree. While in Sydney, she met Nick Austin, whom she married in 2011. They have one child.

3.2.30 Dr Paramjit Singh and Family

Dr Paramjit Singh, MBBS, FRACGP (General Practice), his wife, Dr Rajvinder Kaur (MBBS, FRACGP), and their children, Dr Jasnavaljit Singh (MD) and Darshdeep Kaur, arrived on the Gold Coast in 2016. They had originally left India for New Zealand in 1998 but moved to Australia in 2002 before settling down on the Gold Coast.

Paramjit was born in Nawanshar and completed his matriculation at Doaba Sikh National High School in his hometown. He completed his pre-medical studies at Sikh National College, Banga, and later graduated with a medical degree (anaesthesia) from Dayanand Medical College and Hospital in Ludhiana, India.

Paramjit was an active sportsman in his college years and won third prize in the All-India Medical College five-kilometre marathon. He was also selected as the best athlete and best sportsman in his medical college. Paramjit has maintained his interest in sports by participating in Sikh soccer events and athletics in Australia.

In his capacity as a medical practitioner, Paramjit has acted as medical advisor during the Annual Australian Sikh Games (ANSSACC). He played a role in helping the Brisbane Sikh Games committee initiate the introduction of drug testing for the Sikh Games held in Brisbane in 2012.

As well as sports, Paramjit finds time, between work and family life, to participate in community activities. He was vice-president of the Punjabi Cultural and Sports Association, Brisbane and has been associated with the Brisbane Punjabi Community Calamvale.

Besides these organisations, Paramjit is also founder and president of Better Opportunities Foundation Australia (BOFA), created to raise funds to help provide free education to underprivileged kids in India. He was also involved with the SeaWorld Indian Cultural Night, held in November 2019, to raise charitable funds for the Indian Heritage Group.

Paramjit is currently a foundation member and committee member of the Gold Coast Sikh Association and has been one of the moving forces behind the acquisition of the Gurdwara Sahib Gold Coast in Nerang. This included donating and raising funds, getting Gold Coast City Council approval and identifying engineers for town-planning purposes. He has held the position of Vice-President of the Gold Coast Sikh Association since 2018. Paramjit was one of the doctors who voluntarily provided his expertise in a free medical-examination event at the Nerang Gurdwara.

Dr Rajvinder Kaur achieved her Fellowship in General Practice in 2012 and since then has been working as a full-time general practitioner. She is also employed with Queensland Health in women's health matters.

Paramjit and Rajvinder are the owners of general practice medical centres in Palm Beach and Elanora, which they run in partnership with a second party. They also run their own general practice medical centre in Nerang. They provide free medical services and advice to Indian students and their families, especially those without Medicare or insurance.

Paramjit's family stay closely in touch with his parents, Mr Lehmbar Singh and Mrs Gurdeep Kaur, and his siblings, Amarjit Singh, Jaswinder Singh and Baljit Kaur, who live in Brisbane.

Paramjit and Rajvinder's son, Dr Jasnavaljit Singh, graduated from Bond University with a medical degree in 2018, while their daughter, Darshdeep Kaur, is currently studying medicine, also at Bond. Like her father, Darshdeep is sports-minded and is especially keen on soccer. She plays for a women's soccer club in Robina and a women's team for the Brisbane Punjabi Community Club Calamvale. She was the vice-captain of the winning soccer team in the 2018 Sydney Sikh Games and of the runners-up team in the 2019 Melbourne Sikh Games.

3.2.31 The Sandhu Family

Surjit Singh Sandhu, his wife, Sawinder Kaur Sandhu, and their two teenage daughters, Anisha Kaur Sandhu, 17, and Savina Kaur Sandhu, 14, are the newest of all the individuals and families mentioned in this book. They arrived on the Gold Coast from Gravesend in England in August 2019, having been attracted by the quality of life, weather and the great outdoors that they had experienced on an earlier visit to Australia.

In England, Surjit worked as a gas technician with British Gas while Sawinder was a teaching assistant at a local primary school. Their daughters attended the Mayfield Girls Grammar School in Gravesend. Culturally diverse Gravesend was home to them for a long time and they were comfortably ensconced in a neighbourhood with a thriving Sikh community boasting one of the largest Gurdwaras in Europe. Yet, Surjit says they relish the prospect of living far removed from the heavy industrial environment that surrounded them there.

The family has speedily become part of the Gold Coast Sikh community and tries to participate in as many religious and social activities as possible. Unlike many immigrants who become reclusive upon moving to a new country because of cultural and language differences, Surjit and his family have had no such issues because of their background in England.

This trait, coupled with their enthusiasm to learn about their new home as quickly as possible and the warm welcome they received by the hospitable and supportive Sikh community, has helped them settle in more quickly than most.

At present, Savina attends Assisi Catholic College in Upper Coomera and, to her credit, has already been chosen as a representative for the school council, despite having been enrolled only recently at the school. Anisha is currently awaiting her school results and is aiming for a career in medicine.

4 Formation of the Gold Coast Sikh Association (GCSA)

Nanak, the whole world is in distress.
He who believes in the Name,
Becomes victorious.

Guru Nanak Dev Ji

At the beginning of the 21st century, the Sikh diaspora on the Gold Coast consisted mainly of migrants from India, with a sprinkling of residents who had arrived from countries like Malaysia, Singapore, Kenya and England, who, collectively, were more or less the same size in number as the Indians. However, Sikh migrants from India today far outstrip those from other countries.

The story of the Gold Coast Sikh Association began in 2005. Based on available anecdotal evidence, roughly 25 to 30 Sikh families were living on the Gold Coast in 2005. Prior to 2005, they rarely found the opportunity to mingle on a regular basis – socialising was restricted to occasional parties and house visits. As there was no Gurdwara on the Gold Coast, most of them tended to drive approximately an hour north to Brisbane to meditate at the Logan Road Gurdwara (which at that time was the sole Gurdwara in Brisbane), south to the Murwillumbah Sikh Temple, or even farther away to the Guru Nanak Sikh Temple in Woolgalga. Alternatively, prayers were held in the homes of locals like Patwant Singh Calais and Dr Jagat Jit Ahluwalia Singh.

There had been a proposal for a Gurdwara to be located on the Gold Coast, but the idea was not fully supported at first because the Gold Coast Sikh community was too small to warrant having its own place of assembly. However, with the coaxing of a couple of Malaysian Sikhs (Professor Bee Chen Goh and her husband, Chamkaur Singh Gill), the notion of the Gold Coast Sikh community's own place of worship started to take shape. A meeting room was booked at the Robina Community Centre through the Gold Coast City Council and, on 11 June 2005, the very first Gurdwara-structured Sikh meditation assembly on the Gold Coast was held, with Bhajan Singh Bains leading the prayers and sermons.

Although the assembly comprised only around 30 people and *langgar* was nothing more than tea and biscuits, it proved to be a significant event as it paved the way for regular monthly and bi-monthly assemblies. Over time, these assemblies saw increasing numbers of attendees.

For about five years, Bee Chen and Chamkaur took on the responsibility of holding assemblies informally, with the assistance of a few *sevadaars* (service-oriented participants), including Kuldip Singh Kaurah, Mokhtiar Singh, Patwant Singh Calais, Sanjiv Singh Gill and Jagmohanbir Singh Dillon. Kuldip, Mokhtiar, Sanjiv, Patwant and Chamkaur made sure that the meditation hall, kitchen and *langgar* hall were all set up for the assemblies, while Jagmohanbir played the tabla throughout the hymn-singing sessions, with the assistance of Gobind Singh, who also played the harmonium. The Guru Granth Sahib Ji formed the basis of all the prayers and hymns conducted at each assembly. Bhajan Singh Bains, together with his son Gobind Singh Bains, looked after the transportation of his own copy of the Guru Granth Sahib Ji to the prayer hall for each assembly and ensured that reverential protocol was followed. Essential paraphernalia like microphones, speakers and speaker-stands were looked after by Kuldip Singh Kaurah.

Both adults and children from the *sanggat* participated in hymn-singing. Among the regular child hymn-singers were Jasleen Kaur, Daman

Singh Kaurah and Jasdip Singh Kaurah, while Gobind Singh Bains, Dr Kuljit Singh, Dr Jagat Jit Ahluwalia Singh, Bhajan Singh Bains, Deepa Kaur Calais Pasricha, Raminder Singh Sahota, Dr Hashmita Bagga and Dr Hargurdip Singh were the main adult hymn-singers.

To ensure that the community centre carpets were protected from wear and tear during assemblies, cover sheets were donated by Bhagwan Singh. Kuldip Singh Kaurah was entrusted with ensuring they were looked after and that they were spread over the carpets before each ceremony and removed at the end of the programme. A few members of the community took turns to supply *langgar* at each assembly.

In 2010, the original group of organisers decided that it was time to set up an official organisation to represent all Gold Coast Sikhs. This decision led to the formation of the Gold Coast Sikh Association Incorporated, which was registered with the Queensland Office of Fair Trading in 2010 as a not-for-profit organisation. It became the first official organisation to look after the religious, educational and social interests of the Sikh community on the Gold Coast. The Gold Coast Sikh Association held regular prayer and meditation ceremonies, which included *langgar* sponsored or prepared by various members of the community. The religious assemblies were all scheduled to be held at the Robina Community Centre, with bookings made a year in advance. However, there were a few occasions when the centre became unavailable. When this occurred, services were conducted in the Nerang Bicentennial Community Centre or the new wing of the Robina Community Centre.

The original foundation members of the Gold Coast Sikh Association were Patwant Singh Calais, Dr Jagat Jit Ahluwalia Singh, Mokhtiar Singh, Jagmohanbir Singh Dillon, Kuldip Singh Kaurah, Amarjeet Singh Ahlavadi, Manmohan Singh Bagga and Chamkaur Singh Gill. At its first annual general meeting, a management committee was formed with Patwant Singh Calais as president, Dr Jagat Jit Ahluwalia Singh as vice-president, Mokhtiar Singh as secretary and Kuldip Singh Kaurah as treasurer. In addition, there were nine other committee members, to form a total of 13 committee members. A membership drive was conducted over the next few days to register ordinary members, life members and honorary members.

The presidents who followed Patwant were Kuldip Singh Kaurah (2012–13), Dr Jagat Jit Ahluwalia Singh (2013–14), Chamkaur Singh Gill (2014–15), Mokhtiar Singh (2015–17), Jagmohanbir Singh Dillon (2017–18) and Dr Randhir Singh Mutti (2018 to the time of writing).

One of the initiatives during the presidency of Patwant Singh Calais was the commencement of formal Gurmukhi classes in 2011 under the auspices of the Gold Coast Sikh Association, the first time such classes had ever been held on the Gold Coast. The association rented rooms at Robina State School and evening sessions were conducted by Guru Granth Sahib Ji Academy from Brisbane. Classes for beginners and advanced learners were held once a week under the tutelage of Kamaljit Kaur and Ranjit Singh. Lessons ranged from learning the basics of Gurmukhi to understanding the teachings of the Sikh Gurus.

5

Activities and Responsibilities of the Gold Coast Sikh Association (GCSA)

I bow at His Feet constantly
And pray to him, the Guru.
The True Guru
Has shown me the way.

Guru Nanak Dev Ji

The Gold Coast Sikh Association was authorised to pursue, as one of its objectives upon its incorporation, the establishment of an educational centre for the teaching of languages, culture and religion.

In the early days before securing its own building, the Gold Coast Sikh Association's Gurdwara assemblies were held on a monthly or fortnightly basis in rented rooms at the Robina Community Centre or the Nerang Bicentennial Community Centre. Since securing its own premises in 2018, and with the encouragement of the current president, Dr Randhir Singh Mutti and the committee, the association has instituted weekly assemblies (every Sunday), with provisions in place for the Gurdwara Sahib Gold Coast to be open to members and the public seven days a week. In keeping with the tenets of Sikhism, the door is also open to non-Sikhs to participate if they so wish.

Besides meditation, the Gurdwara also has the resources to conduct special functions like *Amrit Sanchar* ceremonies. The first function in this category was held in 2008, before the establishment of Gurdwara Sahib Gold Coast. It was carried out at the Robina Town Centre for a baby, Jayvir Singh, the son of Sanjiv Singh Gill and Surinder Kaur Gill. The ceremony was conducted by Bhajan Singh Bains. Other activities include studying Sikh scriptures and learning how to play sermon-based musical instruments like the harmonium and tabla.

A major event that was held by the Gold Coast Sikh Association was the Guru Nanak Dev Ji 550th *Gurpurab* (birthday) on 12 November 2019, with prayers and hymn-singing conducted in honour of the founder of Sikhism. This occasion, one of the most important in the Sikh calendar, was commemorated at the Nerang Gurdwara Sahib Gold Coast, with *langgar* served throughout the day.

The Gurudwara Sahib will be OPEN ALL DAY, with Langar service throughout the day.

GURUDWARA SAHIB NERANG
(the gurudwara by the Sangat, for the sangat)
5 Palings Crt, Nerang
EXIT 69

On a social front, fundraising activities like dinner and cultural events are held from time to time. A major annual event in the early years was Desi Night, a dinner and dance event that helped raise much-required funds.

More recently, a Bollywood-style dinner was held at Krish Indian Restaurant, a very popular Gold Coast restaurant, on 29 February 2020. The owner and head chef, Mrs Devi Prasad, generously donated half the restaurant's takings for the event, plus her personal contribution. She deposited a total of $1150.25 into the bank account of the Gold Coast Sikh Association. Krish Indian Restaurant's links with the Gold Coast Sikh Association go back to the early days of the association when Devi regularly and unhesitatingly donated food for fundraising events like Desi Night. She has been known to extend similar charitable gestures to other organisations, such as the Gold Coast Hindu Cultural Association, to which Krish Indian Restaurant has been donating food for the *Navratri* (an Autumn Hindu festival) function for the last eight years.

As enshrined in its constitution, the Gold Coast Sikh Association works to provide community services in the form of donating food, clothing and books, among other items, to the needy. One instance of community service was the conducting of free medical examinations at the Nerang Gurdwara. The doctors who gave their time and expertise to diagnose and advise those who presented themselves for checkups were Dr Maninder Singh, Dr Paramjit Singh and Dr Hargurdip Singh, with a few volunteers filling out relevant documents. In addition, the association conducted an exercise to provide free immigration advice to visiting tourists and international students who had plans to make Australia their home. Adeline Yap-Singh, Moktiar Singh's wife, took time off work to provide this service. Such forms of *seva* encompass the Sikh concept of *mahn*, whereby knowledge and intellectual aptitude are applied to help the less fortunate.

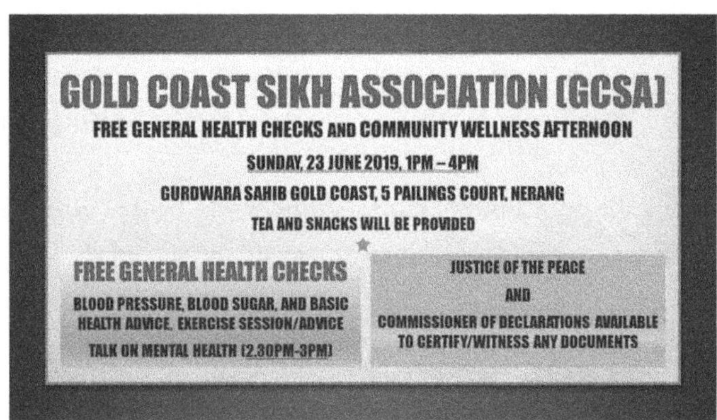

The association also participates in fundraising drives to assist victims of natural disasters like floods, forest fires and pandemics, to reflect the Sikh principles of *dhahn seva* (service via financial assistance) and *tahn seva* (helping through physical service). One such occasion was a fundraising event, held on 23 February 2020, to help victims of bushfires that had engulfed large areas of Australia in late 2019 and early 2020. The event was in the form of a garage sale and raffle of items donated by the community and was helmed by Dr Prabhjot Kaur Singh and her husband, Dr Maninder Singh. A sum of $4000 was raised and a document related to this initiative was handed over to representatives of the Mudgeeraba Rural Fire Brigade during an assembly at the Gurdwara Sahib Gold Coast, Nerang, before the amount was deposited into the bank account of the fire brigade.

Shortly after the forest fires died down, the 2020 Covid-19 pandemic struck the entire world and proved to be a massive challenge for the Gold Coast Sikh Association – a challenge that was met with altruism and resilience. All the members of the association's committee immersed themselves voluntarily and willingly in charitable relief *seva* of a magnitude that most had never been involved in before. They worked tirelessly, in the true spirit of *tahn seva* and *mahn seva*, to deliver comfort to those affected most seriously.

In tandem with the Australia Indian Club Incorporated, Turbans 4 Australia, Khalsa Aid Australia and local Indian restaurants The Tandoori Place, Indian Hut and Delhi Darbar, the association went out of its way to assist those affected by lockdowns and job losses, the elderly, international students, and the needy, regardless of religion, ethnicity or status, by providing them with vegetarian meals. These meals were supplied, free of charge, by Surjit Singh Dhillon, Manmohan Singh Bagga and Amarjeet Singh Ahlawadi, the owners of the aforementioned restaurants.

Volunteers like Jaswinder Singh Gill, Inder Miglani, Harman Sandhu, and Brijesh Patel made themselves available not only to pack meals at the Gurdwara Sahib Gold Coast, but also to make deliveries at various hours of the day to those unable to travel to Nerang. In addition, the secretary of the Gold Coast Sikh Association, Mokhtiar Singh, took on the responsibility of collaborating with Queensland Police to deliver snacks, pickles and tea to 200 Australians of Indian background who were quarantined at the Voco Hotel Gold Coast for two weeks. The food was generously supplied by Khalsa Aid Australia. Mokhtiar was ably supported and assisted in this charitable task by Sam Narayan, the Queensland Police Liaison Officer.

The Gold Coast Sikh Association also delivered free vegetarian meals to the Gold Coast Hospital and Robina Hospital as a token of appreciation for the tireless work done by local health services and frontline medical staff.

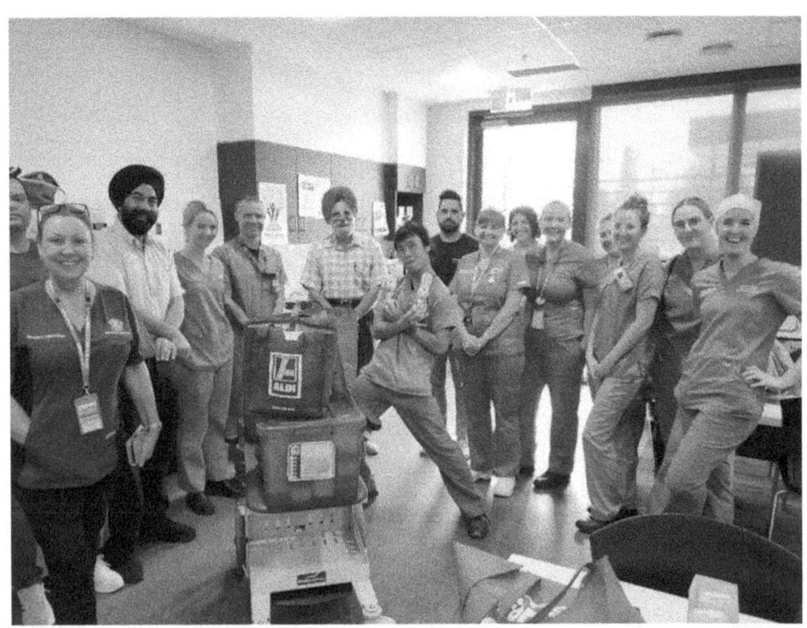

Once more, the Australian Indian Club and Turbans 4 Australia proved to be invaluable with their supply of provisions, complemented by food preparation services from Surjit Singh Dhillon, Manmohan Singh Bagga and Amarjeet Singh Ahlavadi. In addition, Khalsa Aid supplied the Gold Coast Sikh Association with one hundred grocery kits for distribution, free of charge, to deserving families of all religions, national backgrounds and ethnicity and the association took on the responsibility of ensuring that the kits reached them safely. Jaswinder Singh Gill and his team from Australian Indian Club volunteered to carry out this task, picking them up from the Gurdwara Sahib Gold Coast in Nerang and distributing them where they were needed most.

The humanitarian service displayed by all the volunteers during the coronavirus pandemic showcased the Sikh concept of *sarbat da bhela*, meaning 'blessings for everyone'. Their outstanding and selfless dedication was given due recognition in a speech in the Queensland Senate by Senator Paul Scarr, a member of the Liberal National Party of Queensland, in which he praised the work done by Gurdwaras in Brisbane and the Gold Coast, including the Gurdwara Sahib Gold Coast and the Guru Maneyo Granth Gurdwara.

The responsibilities of the Gold Coast Sikh Association include supporting spiritual pursuits through religious, cultural and community activities. In addition, it is geared towards looking after the social welfare of the community by:

- providing marriage guidance and counselling to couples and their families;
- promoting the family unit as a basic social entity that can contribute positively to the country;

- assisting bereaved families and individuals in relation to religious ceremonies and other procedures associated with cremations;
- supporting prison inmates and drug addicts through spiritual guidance, counselling and helping them find jobs upon their release as steps towards reintegrating with society at large; and
- helping families of the seriously ill find relevant medical assistance and organising hospital visits as a source of comfort for patients and their families.

In line with the above, the Gold Coast Sikh Association has held health camps, youth workshops, mental health seminars and domestic violence talks, as well as children's camps in collaboration with Inala Gurdwara in Brisbane.

6

Property Search and the Establishment of a Gurdwara in Nerang by the Gold Coast Sikh Association

There is but One God.
His Name is Truth, He is the Creator
And Immortal His Form.
He is without fear, without enmity, unborn and self-illumined.
By the Guru's Grace, He is obtained.
He was True in the beginning,
He was True when the ages commenced
And has ever been True.
He is also True now.

Guru Nanak Dev Ji

Since the early days of assemblies at the Robina Community Centre, the intention had always been to own a space where the Gold Coast Sikh Association could function officially as a religious, educational and social entity. With the Robina Community Centre being occasionally unavailable due to booking issues and with *sanggat* numbers increasing from year to year, it became quite clear that a property had to be purchased sooner or later.

Concerted efforts to collect funds through donations and special events for this purpose commenced in 2010, with the first Desi Night – a dinner and dance evening involving cultural and social performances held at the Robina Community Centre. Money was raised through ticket sales, a raffle draw and an auction of donated items, among other methods, resulting in a substantial sum of fundraised money from the event.

Nine local restaurateurs generously supplied food free of charge, considerably helping to reduce the cost of organising the event. The restaurateurs were Manmohan Singh Bagga of Indian Hut, Amarjeet Singh Ahlavadi of Delhi Darbar, Sridhar Penumechu of Saffron Restaurant, Jagdish Singh Hayer of Shah Jehan Coolangatta, Surjit Singh Dhillon of Tandoori Place, Bharat and Jyothi Bhushan of Tandoor and Curry Hut, Devi Prasad of Krish Indian, Pushpinder Singh Oberoi of Marigold Restaurant, and Chong and Peggy Lee of Orchid Inn Chinese Restaurant. Additionally, Sridhar Penumechu helped the Gold Coast Sikh Association save money by securing the Robina Community Centre Main Hall expense-free and by decorating the premises to a high level of professionalism free of charge.

Similar functions were held over the next few years, the most recent being in 2017. At the same time, members and non-members, including non-Sikhs, were approached for personal donations and many gave generously. Gurdwaras within Australia (Perth, Brisbane, Sydney, and Melbourne) also assisted in raising funds. A visit to the Johor Bahru Sikh Temple in Malaysia resulted in donations from the *sanggat* of that Gurdwara. In addition, contributions to the *Chedawah* (monetary gifts placed at the altar during each assembly) helped increase the bank balance.

The management committee of the Gold Coast Sikh Association researched the real estate market to find a suitable property to become a long-term place of assembly for members and non-members alike. Various sites around the Gold Coast, including hinterland acreage properties, suburban real estate and industrial buildings, were identified and viewed but were considered unsuitable for a variety of reasons, including distance, suitability and price. These properties included two, in Tallebudgera and Worongary, that the Gold Coast Sikh Association came closest to purchasing. In fact, the association went into contract with the vendors but ended up pulling out of the deals due to one or the other of the reasons mentioned above.

The search for a designated property for a Gurdwara intensified and continued between 2011 and 2018. Eventually, in 2018, a large established building at 5 Palings Court, Nerang, was deemed suitable for purchase. Funds in the bank account of the Gold Coast Sikh Association were topped up with private loans, donations and a bank loan, and the property was purchased and named Gurdwara Sahib Gold Coast. This Gurdwara became the first on the Gold Coast to be completely community-backed and managed by a transparent, community-elected, constitution-based committee – the Gold Coast Sikh Association – and answerable solely to its members.

Major renovations were conducted over the next few months with substantial financial and labour contributions from committee and non-committee members. There were also donations in the form of religious items, electrical goods, television monitors, a closed-circuit television, kitchen equipment, cutlery, crockery and furniture. In the meantime, the association continued with its assemblies at the Robina Community Centre.

The first official prayer and *kirtan* session of the Gold Coast Sikh Association at Gurdwara Sahib Gold Coast was held in one of the designated rooms on 1 January 2019. On 21 April 2019, prayer sessions were permanently moved to the newly renovated Darbar Sahib (main prayer hall).

Since then, the Gurdwara Sahib Gold Coast has held weekly programmes of worship and meditation and provided free *langgar* to Sikhs and non-Sikhs alike. *Langgar* is prepared at other locations and transported to the Gurdwara but once a council-approved kitchen is built in the Gurdwara Sahib, food will be cooked onsite. The management committee is currently in the process of raising funds for a kitchen through donations. In addition, plans are in place to hold regular classes in Gurmukhi and to teach interested parties the rudiments of the harmonium and the tabla with the hope that they will be able to play their part during future religious ceremonies.

7

The Gold Coast Sikh Council (GCSC) and Guru Maneyo Granth Gold Coast Gurdwara

By singing the Guru's hymns,
I, the minstrel spread the Lord's Glory.
Nanak, by praising the True Name,
I have obtained the Perfect Lord.

Guru Nanak Dev Ji

The Gold Coast Sikh Council (GCSC), a registered public charity founded by Surjit Ahluwalia Singh, was formed in 2016. The first Board of Directors of the GCSC included Dr Jagat Jit Ahluwalia Singh, Bhajan Singh Bains and Surjit Ahluwalia Singh.

In late 2016, Surjit Singh informed the Gold Coast and broader Sikh community about the acquisition of a block of land in Helensvale, at 9–11 Shepparton Road, with plans for the construction of the Gold Coast's first purpose-built Sikh Temple and community education centre where Sikhs could come together and learn about Sikhism, the Punjabi language, arts, music and education. On the 10 April 2017, the Gold Coast Sikh Council's proposed plans were approved by the Gold Coast City Council, paving the way for the Gold Coast's history-making Gurdwara to be built.

The site at 9–11 Shepparton Road was cleared on 3 August 2017 to make way for construction and the first-ever *Nee Pathar di Rasam* (ground-breaking ceremony) on the Gold Coast was conducted on 7 October 2017, with Mr Teja Singh, Dr Jagat Jit Ahluwalia Singh, Mr Bhajan Bains, Mr Jagdish (Gajan) Singh Hayer, and Mr Beant Singh as the five main participants *(Punj Pyaye)* in the ceremony.

Tea, juice, water and food was provided to the large number of attendees, whilst Hazoori Raagi from Darbar Sahib Amritsar and Bhai Jagtar Singh sang *kirtan*. Special guest speakers for the event included local Councillor William Owen-Jones and neighbouring Coptic Church priest, Father Abraham.

The construction of the Helensvale Gurdwara commenced in August 2018 after a period of fundraising from local, interstate and international families and Gurdwaras. The contract for the civil works was awarded to Axle Earthworks and the building to iLiv Constructions, who were both enthusiastic about being part of a project that was making history not only for the Sikh community but also for the Gold Coast.

On 11 April 2019, the Gurdwara in Helensvale, formally named the Guru Maneyo Granth Gold Coast Gurdwara, was opened to the community. This momentous occasion commenced with a *Nagar Kirtan* (procession) to the Gurdwara, followed by inaugurating prayers conducted by Bhajan Bains and Dr Jagat Jit Ahluwalia Singh, and the raising of the very first Gold Coast *Nishan Sahib* (Sikh flag), a revered symbol embodying the principles of Sikhism, by Surjit Ahluwalia Singh, General Manager of Gold Coast Sikh Council.

History continued to be made on that day, with the Gold Coast's first official Gurdwara-related *Akhand Paatth* (three-day reading of the Guru Granth Sahib) with tea, sweets and *langgar* available to all congregants. The prayer concluded on 13 April 2019, also marking *Vaisakhi* celebrations at the site. Apart from the many locals who took to the stage, Bhai Hardeep Singh (Ludhiane Wale) and Bhai Karaj Singh (Hazoori Raagi Darbar Sahib Amritsar) provided the attendees with *kirtan* throughout the day.

People from all over Australia and overseas attended the event over the three days. Attendees also included local members of parliament, councillors and members of the Queensland Police and Fire Services.

The Gurdwara also held the first-ever *Gurmat* (teachings of the Guru) camp on the Gold Coast on 21 April 2019, and the first *Anand Karaj* (wedding) ever officiated on the Gold Coast on 20 July 2019.

'Oneness' is a key pillar for the GCSC, and as such, on 28 November 2019, the Gurdwara also held a memorial service for the untimely passing of prominent local cricketer Vikas Malhotra, who was a member of the Hindu community.

The Guru Maneyo Granth Gold Coast Gurdwara serves not only as a Sikh temple but also as a community education centre. It is open seven days a week, has an onsite resident *Granthi* and *Raagi Jatha* (hymn-singing group), provides meals at all open times to attendees, and has education classes and *Gatka* (Sikh martial arts) lessons.

The Guru Maneyo Granth Gurdwara played an important role in supporting the needy during the Covid-19 pandemic in 2020 by providing free drive-through meals from its premises in collaboration with the Biggera Waters and Helensvale branches of Bendigo Bank. Food was made available to everyone, regardless of religious leanings, race or status. This initiative was acknowledged and praised in a speech by Senator Paul Scarr in the Queensland Senate.

An important achievement by Surjit Ahluwalia Singh on behalf of the Guru Maneyo Granth Gurdwara was convincing King's Christian College Gold Coast to alter the school's uniform code so that Sikh students could attend classes with their uncut hair, turbans and bangles intact, thereby furthering awareness about the Sikh religion in the wider Gold Coast community.

The management of the Guru Maneyo Granth Gold Coast Gurdwara is overseen by a board of directors who are ably supported by willing volunteers from the *sanggat* who help to prepare and serve *langgar*, keep the premises clean and tidy and ensure that events and activities proceed smoothly. Although new, the Gurdwara has become very popular with congregants from the Gold Coast, Brisbane and beyond.

8

Conclusion

> Those who have loved are those who have found God.
>
> Guru Nanak Dev Ji

Records point to Sikhs having been part of the Australian landscape since the middle of the nineteenth century. They came as farmhands, horse-drawn cart hawkers, pedlars and cameleers. It was obvious that their original intention was to accumulate enough money to secure a comfortable life for themselves and their families in India when they went back home. However, more and more decided to call Australia home over the years, raising their children to be both Sikh and Australian.

Compared to these early Sikhs who were restricted to working in jobs that required no more than manual toil, Sikhs migrating to Australia these days hold academic, professional and skilled-workforce qualifications.

As far as the Gold Coast is concerned, information about the history of early Sikh migrants appears to be sparse. Details about their presence prior to the 1980s are few and it was not until 1980 that they started making a mark. Since then, they have established themselves in various sectors of the Gold Coast workforce, from medical professionals, restaurateurs and tertiary-level educators, to corporate-business operators, health-care workers and transport personnel. In addition, many young Sikhs have chosen the Gold Coast for tertiary and professional studies, with quite a few going on to secure permanent residency and citizenship after graduating.

Gold Coast Sikh residents of today are mainly from India, but there are some from other parts of the Commonwealth including Malaysia, Singapore, United Kingdom and Kenya.

Sikhs have proven to be very hard-working and economically productive, thereby improving the quality of life of the general populace of the Gold Coast. They have also exhibited their worth during disasters like floods and forest fires that plague the country annually, and through their willingness to come to the aid of those who need it most, no matter the race, religion, gender or status of the victims. This trait of serving selflessly was particularly in evidence when the catastrophic Covid-19 pandemic struck in 2020. Gold Coast and Australian Sikhs were at the forefront, preparing and delivering free food and assistance to those affected by the resultant lockdown in tandem with organisations like Turbans 4 Australia, Khalsa Aid Australia and Australia Indian Club.

As with Sikh communities in other parts of the world, the Gold Coast is more than likely to see an increase in the number of Sikh entrepreneurs, medical professionals, academics, financial planners and advisors, software engineers, and high-level public servants over the coming years. There may even be policy makers at government level, as is the case in Canada and the United Kingdom.

Organisations like Sikh Youth Australia and its offshoot, Young Sikh Professionals Network (YSPN), have an important role to play in the future success of Sikh Gold Coasters and Sikh Australians by giving Sikhs, especially young professionals, a higher profile in society. Given the ease with which they assimilate local values, there is no doubt that future generations of Sikhs will prove to be an asset to the Gold Coast and Australia – they possess the same Sikh ethics of honour, diligence and hard work that the early Sikh pioneers brought with them to Australia. The ever-present traits of these ancestors are best summed up in the poetry of Guru Nanak Dev Ji:

Whatever kind of seed is sown in a field,

Prepared in due season,
A plant of the same kind,
Marked with the unique qualities of the seed,
Springs up in it.

In conclusion, Sikh Australians are very much a part of modern-day Australia and one can safely assume that they would like nothing better than to see the nation blessed in every way, as it moves into a future ripe with hope. The closing line in the *Ardaas* reads, *Nanak Naam Chardi Kala, Tayray Bhaanay Sarbat Da Bhalaa,* which translates to, 'Through Nanak, may your name strengthen and the Spirit be glorified and may you prosper'. The line invokes God's grace on humanity to bless the whole world with peace and prosperity.

III. Migrant: Soul of Dreamtime

An ancient wisdom moves around you,
Of spirits that once enveloped the land.
They softly speak of a life they knew,
Of Nature's blue seas, green trees and red sand.

So, be one with the soul of Dreamtime.
Respect the Earth that nurtured your brother.
Air is the Teacher (message sublime),
Water, the Father and Earth, the Mother.

CS Gill

References

2016 Census QuickStats. (2016). Retrieved June 24, 2020, from https://quickstats.censusdata.abs.gov.au/census_services/getproduct/census/2016/quickstat/SSC14402

Adams, M. (n.d.) Remembering Sikhs in the first AIF. Retrieved June 27, 2020, from https://www.awm.gov.au/articles/blog/remembering-sikhs

Ahmad, F. (2014). In remembrance of Bud. Retrieved June 27, 2020, from https://www.indianlink.com.au/in-remembrance-of-bud/

All About Sikhs. (n.d.). Sikhs in Australia. Retrieved July 8, 2020, from https://www.allaboutsikhs.com/demo/demo

Allen, M. (2008). Chapter 3, 'A fine type of Hindoo' meets 'the Australian type': British Indians in Australia and diverse masculinities. In Desley Deacon, Penny Russel & Angela Woolacott (Eds.), *Transnational Ties: Australian lives in the world.* Retrieved June 28, 2020, from https://press-files.anu.edu.au/downloads/press/p20951/mobile/index.html

Aly, W. (2013, September 18). Historyonics: Otim Singh's general store. Retrieved June 26, 2020, from https://www.abc.net.au/radionational/programmes/drive/historyonics3a-otim-singh27s-general-store/4966552

Arora, A. & Singh, M. K. (2019, April 20). Sikhs contribute $8.1 billion annually to the Australian economy: Report. Retrieved September 15, 2019, from https://www.sbs.com.au/language/english/sikhs-contribute-8-1-billion-annually-to-the-australian-economy-report

Australian Bureau of Statistics. (2018, January 18). Census reveals Australia's religious diversity on World Religion Day. Retrieved January 24, 2020, from https://www.abs.gov.au/AUSSTATS/abs@.nsf/mediareleasesbyReleaseDate/8497F7A8E7DB5BEFCA25821800203DA4?OpenDocument

Australian Sikhs Census 2016. (2016). Retrieved September 14, 2019, from https://www.adsac.com.au/australian-sikhs-census-2016/#comment-29

Australian Sikh Heritage. (2014, September). Nehal Singh, Herman Singh and Sundah Singh. Retrieved June 24, 2020, from https://www.australiansikhheritage.com/nehal-herman-and-sunder-singh/

Bedi, H. S. & Bedi, H. S. (2017). Johnnie the Sikh and their loyal mules.

Retrieved June, 22, 2020, from https://www.sikh.com.au/cgi-bin/index.cgi?page=4

Burke and Wills Web Digital Research Archive. (n.d.). Robert O'Hara Burke's camels. Retrieved July 19, 2019, from www.burkeandwills.net.au/Camels/Burkes_Camels.htm

Coolangatta Estate (n.d.). The Estate: A convict history. Retrieved June 28, 2020, from https://www.coolangattaestate.com.au/history

Copp, A. & Booth, A. (2017, July 26). 'Not many people know about Sikhs': Spotlight on Australia's growing community. Retrieved July 8, 2020 from https://www.sbs.com.au/news/not-many-people-know-about-sikhs-spotlight-on-australia-s-growing-community

Gill, A. S. (2013, April 28). Thoughts on this ANZAC Day. Retrieved July 6, 2020 from http://sikhchic.com/history/thoughts_on_this_anzac_day

Grewal, P. (2016, October 23). Know the story of Massa Singh – Australian Sikh Heritage. Retrieved March 21, 2020, from https://www.sbs.com.au/language/english/audio/know-the-story-of-massa-singh-australian-sikh-heritage

Grewal, P. (2017, February 8). Charting the Sikh connection to Australia's first people. Retrieved August 13, 2019, from https://www.sbs.com.au/yourlanguage/punjabi/en/article/2017/02/08/charting-sikh-connection-australias-first-people

History of Brisbane Sikh Temple. (n.d.) Retrieved June 27, 2020, from https://brisbanesikhtemple.org.au/history-of-brisbane-sikh-temple/

History Teachers' Association of WA. (n.d.). Sikh and Indian Australians: A White Australia. Retrieved August 13, 2019, from http://htawa.net.au/sikh_indian_australians/PDF/SH_Yr6_LS1.pdf

History Teachers' Association of WA. (n.d.). Sikh and Indian Australians: Memories of Baba Ram Singh's Granddaughter. Retrieved June 29, 2020, from www.htawa.net.au/sikh_indian_australians/PDF/SH_Yr6_LS2_TR2.pdf

History Teachers' Association of WA. (n.d.). Sikh and Indian Australians: Stepping into the daily life of the Indian hawker in the Colonies. Retrieved August 13, 2019, from http://htawa.net.au/sikh_indian_australians/PDF/SH_Yr5_LS3.pdf

Jones, B. T. (2017, April 10). Australian politics explainer: The White Australia policy. Retrieved July 12, 2020, from https://theconversation.com/australian-policy-explainer-the-white-australia-policy-74084

Kenna, L. & Jordan, C. (2014a). Australian Sikh and Hindu – Indian wrestlers. Retrieved February 14, 2020, from http://australianindianhistory.com/indian-wrestlers-australia/

Kenna, L. & Jordan, C. (2014b). Dabee Singh a pioneer: One of the earliest arrivals to Australia. Retrieved June 26, 2020, from http://australianindianhistory.com/dabee-singh-a-pioneer/

Kenna, L. & Jordan, C. (2014c). Massa Singh Chahal – Cartage Contractor, hawker, wrestler and athlete. Retrieved June 28, 2020, from http://australianindianhistory.com/massa-singh-cameleer-hawker-wrestler-athlete/

Kenna, L. & Jordan, C. (2015a, January 9). Sikh and Hindu cremations in Australia. Retrieved February 14, 2020,from http://australianindianhistory.com/wp-content/uploads/2018/12/2015-Sikh-and-Hindu-Cremations-in-Australlia-Putarb-Singh-Henty-and-the-Albury-Indian-Cemetery-NSW-PWPAIHSweb.pdf

Kenna, L. & Jordan, C. (2015b, October 3). Dabee Singh a pioneer. Retrieved June 26, 2020, from http://australianindianhistory.com/dabee-singh-a-pioneer/

Kenna, L. & Jordan, C. (2015c, October 3). Pooran Dabee-Singh a pioneer: The son of one of the early pioneers. Retrieved June 26, 2020, from http://australianindianhistory.com/pooran-dabee-singh-a-pioneer

Kenna, L. & Jordan, C. (2016, May 10). Hawkers. Retrieved July 12, 2020, from http://australianindianhistory.com/category/hawkers/page/2/

Kenna, L. & Jordan, C. (2020, January 11). Indian hawkers purchased goods from factories in Melbourne, Victoria. Retrieved June 26, 2020, from http://australianindianhistory.com/indian-hawkers-and-shoe-factories-in-melbourne-victoria/

Lee, T. (2020, March 29). Siva Singh, immigrant who fought White Australia policy to regain right to vote, leaves lasting legacy. Retrieved April 12, 2020, from https://www.abc.net.au/news/2020-03-29/siva-singh-fights-white-australia-policy-for-right-to-vote/12097822

McCarthy, R. G. (2013). The Sikh diaspora in Australia: Migration, multiculturalism and the imaging of home (unpublished doctoral dissertation). University of Pittsburgh, Pittsburgh, Pennsylvania

Merani, K. (2017, June 1). Celebration of Sikhs' contribution to Australia. Retrieved June 22, 2020, from https://www.sbs.com.au/language/english/celebration-of-sikhs-contribution-to-australia

More, A. & Singh, M. (n.d.) Sikh Community at Woolgoolga. Retrieved June 25, 2020, from https://www.sikh.com.au/cgi-bin/index. cgi?page=1

National Archives of Australia (n.d.) The Immigration Restriction Act 1901. Retrieved August 13, 2019, from https://www.naa.gov.au/explore-collection/immigration-and-citizenship/immigration-restriction-act-1901

Our Story. (n.d.). Retrieved June 21, 2020, from https://www.banksa.com.au/about/overview.

Sikh Interfaith Council of Australia. (n.d.). Sikhs in Australia. Retrieved July 18, 2019, from www.sikhinterfaithvic.org.au/sikhsinoz.html

Sikhiwiki contributors. (2018, October 22). Mool Mantar. Retrieved June 30, 2020, from https://www.sikhiwiki.org/index.php/Mool_Mantar

Singh, G. (2020, May 23). Need for early Sikh settlers museum. Retrieved 20 June, 2020, from https://asiasamachar.com/2020/05/23/need-for-early-sikh-settlers-museum/

Singh, M. K. (2014a, April 11). Bud Singh – an inspirational Indian Australian pioneer. Retrieved February 14, 2020, from https://www.sbs.com.au/language/english/audio/bud-singh-a-inspirational-indian-australian-pioneer

Singh, M. K. (2014b, December 22). The Bud who came into bloom. Retrieved February 14, 2020, from https://www.theindiansun.com.au/2014/12/22/the-bud-who-came-into-bloom-first-punjabis-in-australia/

Singh, M. K. (2017, June 30). Sikhism is now the fifth largest religion in Australia. Retrieved September 3, 2019, from https://www.sbs.com.au/yourlanguage/punjabi/en/article/2017/06/30/sikhism-now-fifth-largest-religion-australia

Singh, M. K. (2018a, January 18). There is a land of five rivers called Punjaub – right here in Australia. Retrieved August 13, 2019, from https://www.sbs.com.au/language/english/there-is-a-land-of-five-rivers-called-punjaub-right-here-in-australia

Singh, M. K. (2018b, January 19). This is how the Australian Punjaub got its name. Retrieved August 13, 2019, from https://www.sbs.com.au/language/english/this-is-how-the-australian-punjaub-got-it-s-name

Singh, M. K. (2018c, July 13). Sikhs explore their 120-year-old connection with Indigenous Australians. Retrieved September 3, 2019, from https://www.sbs.com.au/language/english/sikhs-explore-their-120-year-old-connection-with-indigenous-australians

Spennemann, D. H. R. (2019). Suicides of Punjabi hawkers in 19th – and early 20th – century Australia. *Indian Journal of Psychology, 61*(4), 347-351. Retrieved July 11, 2020, from https://www.ncbi.nlm.nih.gov/pmc/articles/PMC6657551/

Staley, M. (2015, December 8). Sikh farmhands. Retrieved June 21, 2020, from https://greataustralianstory.com.au/story/sikh-farmhands

Tewari, A. (2014, September 26). From Amritsar to Australia: Punjabi migration trends. Retrieved July 8, 2020, from https://www.indianlink.com.au/from-amritsar-to-australia-punjabi-migration-trends/

Wikipedia contributors. (n.d.). Indian Australians. In *Wikipedia, The Free Encyclopedia*. Retrieved August 20, 2019, from https://en.wikipedia.org/wiki/Indian_Australians

Wikipedia contributors. (n.d.). Sikhism. In *Wikipedia, The Free Encyclopedia.* Retrieved June 14, 2020, from https://en.wikipedia.org/wiki/Sikhism

Wikipedia contributors. (n.d.). Sikhism in Australia. In *Wikipedia, The Free Encyclopedia.* Retrieved March 11, 2020, from https://en.wikipedia.org/wiki/Sikhism_in_Australia

Wikipedia contributors. (n.d.). Woolgoolga, New South Wales. In *Wikipedia, The Free Encyclopedia.* Retrieved June 17, 2020, from https://en.wikipedia.org/wiki/Woolgoolga,_New_South_Wales

Wood, J. (2018, September 30). Buttan Singh's clubs. Retrieved June, 29, 2020 from https://www.oldtimestrongman.com/blog/2018/09/30/buttan-singhs-clubs/

Printed in Australia
AUHW021030271120
337934AU00005BA/23

9 781922 454188